MOCK
THE
WEEK'S
FUNNIEST
BOOK OF
ALL TIME

First published 2011 by Boxtree
an imprint of Pan Macmillan, a division of Macmillan Publishers Limited
Pan Macmillan, 20 New Wharf Road, London N1 9RR
Basingstoke and Oxford
Associated companies throughout the world
www.panmacmillan.com

ISBN 978-0-75222-741-2

9 8 7 6 5 4 3 2 1

A CIP catalogue record for this book is available from
the British Library.

Photos © Shutterstock
Design by Estuary English
Printed and bound in Italy by Printer Trento S.r.l.

EWAN PHILLIPS, DAN PATTERSON, SIMON BULLIVANT,
ROB COLLEY, DAN GASTER, GED PARSONS, GILES PILBROW,
STEVE PUNT AND COLIN SWASH

BOXTREE

CONTENTS

6 UNLIKELY TUBE STATIONS

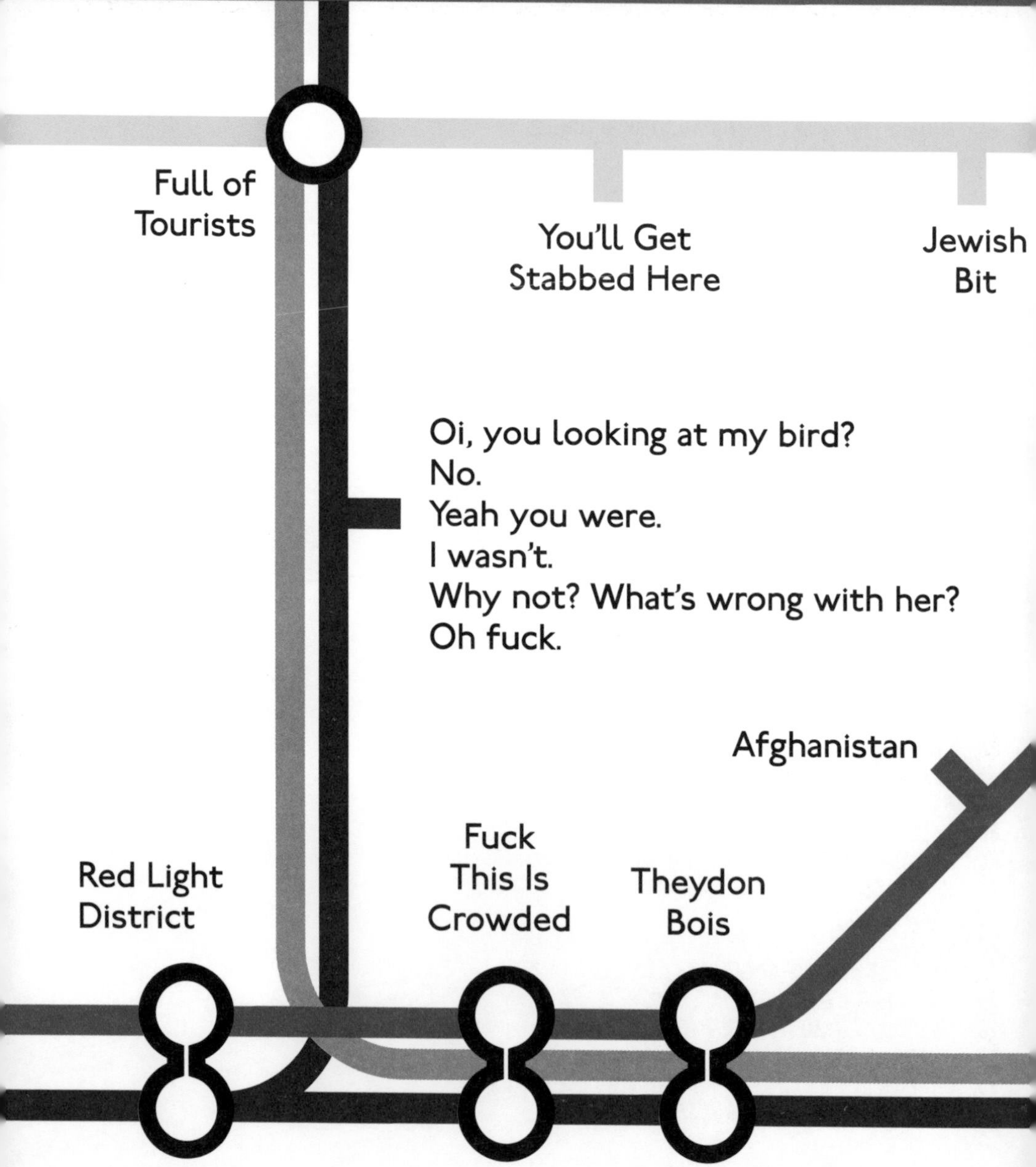

Full of Tourists

You'll Get Stabbed Here

Jewish Bit

Oi, you looking at my bird?
No.
Yeah you were.
I wasn't.
Why not? What's wrong with her?
Oh fuck.

Afghanistan

Red Light District

Fuck This Is Crowded

Theydon Bois

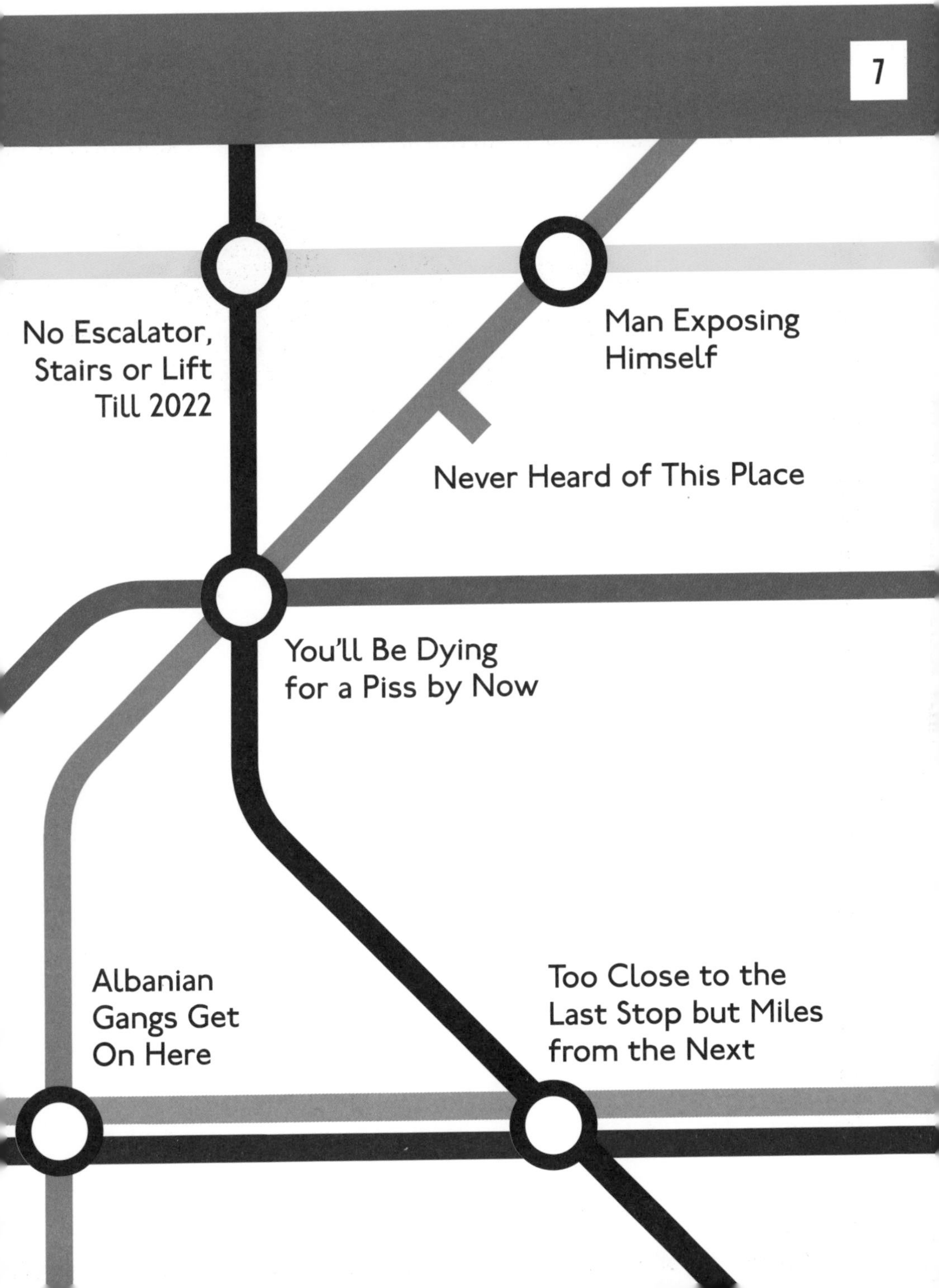

No Escalator, Stairs or Lift Till 2022

Man Exposing Himself

Never Heard of This Place

You'll Be Dying for a Piss by Now

Albanian Gangs Get On Here

Too Close to the Last Stop but Miles from the Next

THINGS YOU WOULDN'T READ

CHAPTER 3

'THE THING IS, Anne,' said George thoughtfully, 'I think I'm not so much a tomboy, as a lesbian...'

Christopher Robin asked Eeyore why he was depressed. 'You should be happy,' he said, 'with the size of that cock.'

It wasn't a great day for Budgie the Helicopter as he was shot down by the Taliban.

After living under the hill for several months Mr Fox thought, 'Sod this, I'm going to move to the city and eat out of some bins.'

As they opened the wardrobe door they saw Aslan parading around in Mummy's dress.

'Who's been eating *my* porridge?' said the promiscuous gay.

The Gruffalo walked on through the wood, but even he was afraid of the old man with no buttons on his raincoat.

And they all lived happily ever after – except for Raoul Moat.

CHILDREN'S BOOK

Gently, tenderly, he undid Miss Tiggywinkle's bra…

'The sky is *not* falling, Chicken Licken, you've just dropped a tab of acid.'

And Thomas the Tank Engine stayed in all day, because it was the wrong kind of snow.

'Hello', said Rupert, 'have you seen Bill the Badger?'
'Yes, follow those double white lines on the A338 and you'll find him in no time.'

Little Miss Sex Slave lived in a grubby flat near Baker Street.

'Well done the Famous Five, looks like we've seen off that gypsy encampment, thanks to those lashings of petrol bombs! Hurray!'

The children were disappointed to learn that Aslan was now dancing for money in a Romanian circus.

Peter Rabbit felt a bit sick, he had been forced to smoke 400 Benson & Hedges.

It was then that she saw Black Beauty (page 18 of the Ann Summers catalogue).

Once inside the Gingerbread House Hansel and Gretel were imprisoned in a special gingerbread basement that the Austrian witch had made.

As they chased the smugglers across the motorway, Timmy was a bit slow and the Famous Five became Four.

10 UNLIKELY THINGS TO HAVE HEAR

'What a sight! Kate Middleton steps out in beautiful Alexander McQueen with the sun resplendent behind her, clearly revealing her lacy white panties and the outline of her bra.'

'I, William, take thee, Pippa ... sorry, Catherine...'

'And the Queen there, smiling. She's listening to the 2.15 at Fontwell Park, where her crafty each-way has just romped home at 50–1.'

'Heads of state from all over the world here: President Sarkozy of France ... Angela Merkel there ... Colonel Gaddafi and Robert Mugabe sharing a joke...'

'And there's Mrs Middleton, looking at her daughter at the altar and trying desperately not to think about her with a mouthful of Royal cock.'

'And Princess Beatrice there, looking radiant in a really fucking stupid hat.'

'Now we come to the traditional trying on of the glass slipper, which is being brought up the aisle as ever by Buttons.'

'And a fight breaks out in the Abbey as Gareth Thomas stamps on Mike Tindall's fingers in a race for the bar...'

'As I watch the ring being put on the finger it's time to welcome viewers joining us here on BBC Two. Viewers on BBC One can watch *Doctors* followed by *Diagnosis Murder*.'

'Kate Middleton looks radiant as she gets out of the carriage, with her sparkling white dress and beautiful smile. Fingers crossed she's not on the blob.'

'And now, the archbishop asks if anyone knows any just cause why these two should not be joined in holy matrimony ... we have the traditional wait while six nutters outline their rightful claims to the throne based on being descended from the two princes in the tower.'

'Shit! Harry's dad's outside causing trouble again.'

'The happy couple pose for *OK!* magazine and brandish the chocolate bar they're promoting with Myleene Klass.'

'And now for the readings, beginning with a poem written specially for the occasion by the Poet Laureate and read by Kerry Katona.'

'William, dressed in the colours of the Irish Guards, Harry in the uniform of the Waffen SS...'

'And now, before the exchanging of the rings, it's time for the comparison of the tattoos.'

'People say Kate is too common to marry a prince but I think arriving wearing a pink dress in a golden pumpkin is entirely fitting.'

'Here to sing "Don't Go Breaking My Heart" - Elton John!'

'Do you, Kate, give up your sanity, privacy and ambitions to take this man who, whilst nowhere near as good-looking as when you met, will, if his dad's anything to go by, be knocking off some other sort with a quadruple-barrelled name by 2014?'

'And as we look at the beautiful pair walking down the aisle, it's difficult to imagine them ever being parted - but enough about Pippa's buttocks, here come Wills and Kate.'

12 BAD TITLES FOR LOVE SONGS

'Jizz On My Pillow'

'Stop! In the Name of Christ'

'Can't Get Enough of Your Love, Dave'

'Is This the Way to East Croydon?'

'Truly, Madly, Creepy'

'You've Lost That Feeling (In Your Legs)'

'Prisoner in My Basement'

'Sitting on the Dick of a Gay'

'You Can't Hurry Lunch'

'Just the Three of Us'

'Bit Higher, Yes, Not Up There'

'I Love You More Than Gabriel Agbonlahor'

'You Make Me Come Out in a Rash'

'Who's the Bastard in the Black?'

DO YOU
DO YOU
DO YOU
SIDE A
45 RPM
MOUTH PARTY RECORDS
MADE IN THE EU
WANNA SUCK
MY KNOB?

14 UNLIKELY CROSSWORD CLUES

Across

1. Length of my penis in inches (3)
2. The word 'badger' (6)
3. Footballer with a court injunction preventing me from selling my story to the *News of the World* (5, 6)
4. Pub I used to go to in Bolton (3, 6)
5. Underworked postman, just three letters.
6. That stuff, you know (6)
7. Sc*nthorpe loses Shorpe to find Piers Morgan (4)
8. Alzheimer's. Blank, blank, blank, blank, blank.
9. Fuck you. You Twat (1)
10. Free the Birmingham (6)
11. How do you know this is a proper clue? (17, 453)
12. Two for tea and tea for (2)

Down

1. Queen swallowed semen, I hear (2, 4)
2. Snow White and the (7 Dwarves)
3. ‘Hello, Ian. Is that a - - - - -?’ (5)
4. Small cottage, two up, two down.
5. Skin I have on the end of my knob (4)
6. You won’t get this (12, 4, 3, 5)
7. Me in my school photo, three across, two down.
8. Four plus one perhaps (4)
9. Hell-*lo*, ding dong! (36, 24, 36)
10. What did you have for your tea last night?
11. Dunking scrotum in someone’s mouth when asleep (3, 7)
12. For Christ’s sake get a (4)
13. Crossword compiler’s next job (7). Oh great, thanks very much.
14. DNA (three letters)

16 STRANGE THINGS TO HEAR FROM

'In one hundred yards, turn left ... it's a nice day, we could have a cuddle in the lay-by.'

'Turn left ... at the Chinky.'

'Did you turn the gas off? Did you lock the front door? Did you? I don't think you did. Should we go back?'

'In fifty yards veer left and run over that murderous fox.'

'Enemies of the – Daleks – must – be – ex – ter – minated!'

'Sorry, back to where you started, I've got the map upside down.'

'Pull into the next services, I'm busting for a piss.'

'You know who used to live round here? Deirdre's boyfriend's family. Of course they've moved to Dorset now ... hang on, we've missed the turning.'

'You never take me anywhere nowadays.'

'Ooh, stop! Look, DFS have got a sale on.'

'Travel for one hundred miles, complete a U-turn and travel for one hundred miles. It's right behind you.'

'In fifty yards, dogging opportunity on your right.'

'Don't leave me. I saw you looking at that iPad.'

'You are driving in the wrong gear, and those shorts and sandals look ridiculous.'

'Re-calculating route ... Idiot, now LISTEN this time.'

'It's left ... no, right! Oh I don't know, stop shouting.'

'Harrumph, well, I'm surprised you don't know the way to your mother's house, we seem to go there often enough.'

'I don't recognize anything round here, it's all changed ... didn't that used to be a garage?'

'You have reached your destination. I see it's the off-licence. Again.'

'To rid yourself of pursuing agents, first deploy oil slick dispenser, then twin machine guns and if necessary drive off pier and turn car into submarine.'

UNLIKELY THINGS TO READ IN A

INSTRUCTIONS

- Plugging in this toaster and leaving it by the side of the bath will save you valuable time in the morning.
- When attaching the plug remember the red wire is live ... or is it the blue one?
- Don't try and follow the drawings, they are just there as decoration.
- The following instructions are meant for women only – men, just plug it in and start pressing buttons at random.
- Thank you for buying our Frömstå table. Instructions: slide under food.
- If you took more than twenty minutes to get this instruction manual out of the plastic wrapper, good luck with this latest computer.
- Congratulations on overpaying for this brand-name DVD player!
- In the absence of a foreskin, go to figure 3.
- Thank you for buying this digital radio. If you experience muffled sound and inconsistent signal strength it's working perfectly.
- 1. Attach Point 2 to Hole 3 and repeat with 3 and 4. Pause. Realize this can't be right. Shout: 'Fucking stupid thing!!'
- Place tip of finger (fig 3) on clitoris (fig 4). What do you mean she hasn't got one?

1. Press 'on' button.
Got that? No?
Fuck me. Are you sure
you're up to this?
ON / OFF

20 BAD THINGS TO HEAR AT WORK

'Well, you've shown me the restroom and the warehouse, but where do I masturbate?'

'I think there was a bit missing on the fax that came through. I thought I was joining a "laughter house" not a "slaughter house".'

'Sod the tea break, where's the bar?'

'I told you I'd get promoted if I sucked the boss off.'

'Right, which of these chairs do I sit in, I haven't flown one of these big planes before.'

'Well, that seems pretty simple: launch nukes, self destruct ... no, hang on...'

'I don't much like the look of this dump. Still, I'll be moving on soon, anyway.'

'I thought, seeing as they're dead, it didn't really matter what we did with them.'

'Just to let you know, I've already labelled all my biscuits ... individually.'

'The photocopier's broken down so I'm going to show you what my arse looks like.'

'I realize the company has a "no smoking" policy, but can I still do crack?'

'Hello, class – I'm Mr Johnson – and I'm living proof that the police background check can't catch everyone.'

'I can't believe it! – caught stealing buns on my first day at the baker's. But frankly it's your own fault for employing an elephant in the first place.'

22 UNLIKELY TITLES FOR MEMOIRS

A CLEGG UP: Nick Clegg

PUTIN' IT DOWN ON PAPER: Vladimir Putin

INSERT PAGE 1 (SMERVIE) INTO PAGE 2 (FLAAF) AND READ: by the bloke who invented IKEA

THE UNEDITED DIARIES VOL. 1: Elton Welsby

THE CABLE GUY: Vince Cable

BY-ÖPIK: LEMBIT ÖPIK

CHEEKY FUCKER! LEMBIT ÖPIK: THE BIOGRAPHY

CAN WE FORGET ABOUT THE USA GAME NOW: Robert Green

MORE THAN JUST A PRETTY FACE: Angela Merkel

TO THE MANOR OSBOURNE: George Osbourne

WHO'S THE DADDY?: Prince Harry

THE COLOUR PURPLE: Autobiography of Alex Ferguson's Face

POSTCARDS FROM THE SPARE ROOM: Selected Poems of Ryan Giggs

Silvio Berlusconi

Adventures with my knob

UNLIKELY THINGS TO READ IN

One of the telltale signs of pregnancy is a head poking out of the vagina.

Put your head between your knees – you might be able to suck your own cock, and that should take your mind off your nosebleed.

If the patient has swellings to the chest, it *could* be a girl, in which case you've got about four minutes for a rummage before the ambulance arrives.

To impress the ambulance driver shout out 'She's 40 over 60' and then melt into the background.

Do you note any of the following: sweating, hands shaking, racing pulse? Well, fat lot of good you're going to be.

If you suspect that the patient has had a heart attack, he's out of luck – we don't cover that until book two.

The patient may be suffering from contusion, or do I mean confusion. Oh, now *I'm* contused.

If you're struggling to loosen the patient's clothing, make sure they're not lying on their front.

If passageway is blocked, use finger. Then check the patient's mouth.

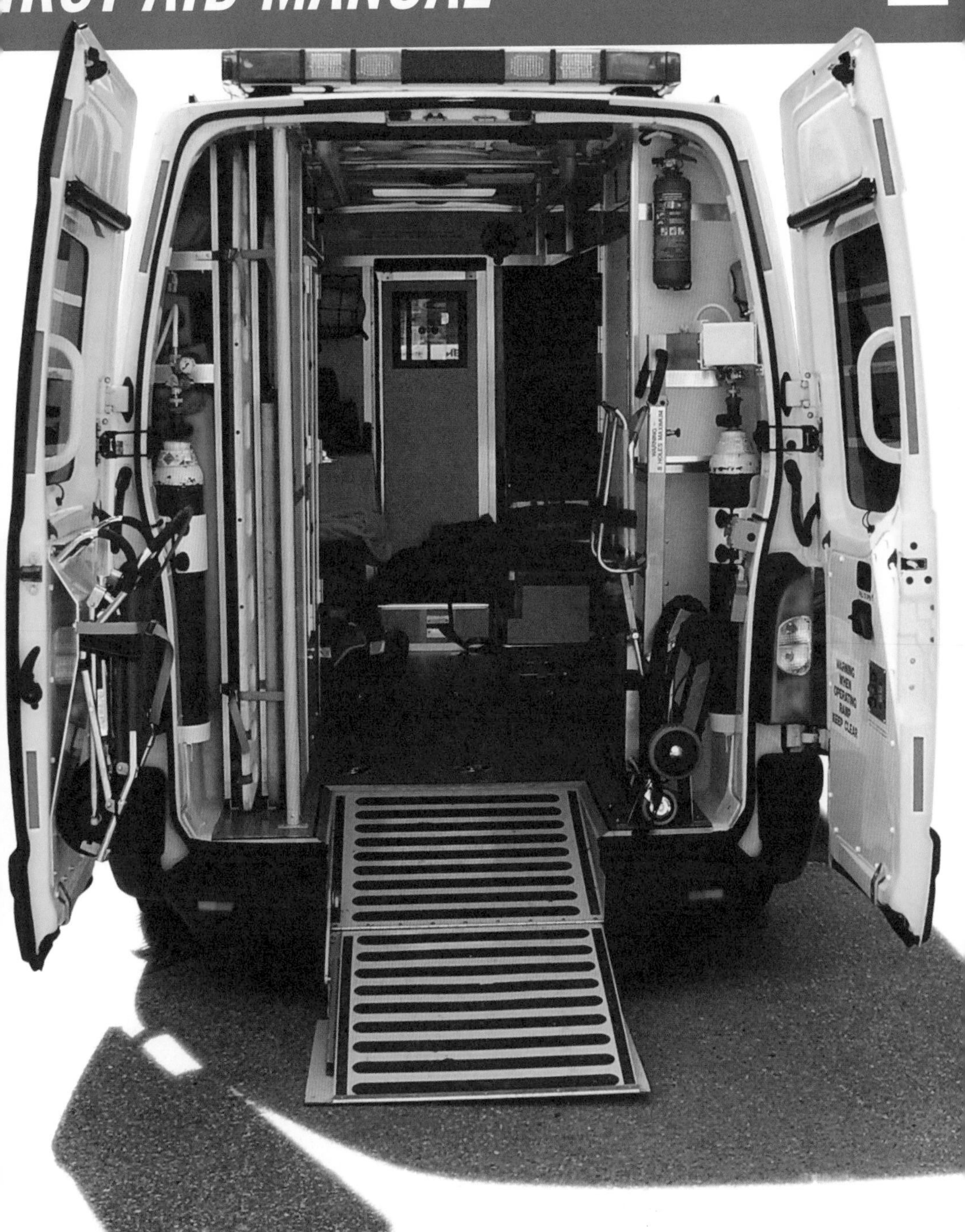
WARNING
WHEN
OPERATING
RAMP
KEEP CLEAR

26 UNLIKELY HOROSCOPES

Your Stars

By our expert Astrologer

Cancer, a doubly unlucky day as you will get cancer AND crabs.

The one problem for you today is money. You may be disappointed with a purchase. Maybe a newspaper with a really shit horoscope in.

All Sagittarians will get a blow-job today. Well, I'll do my best. First come first served.

Today there'll be a really amazing ... call my hotline now to hear the rest of this incredible horoscope.

Mercury is very present in your house, so make sure you boil all your drinking water.

Right, that's it, suckers! I've finally made enough money and I'm retiring. This is all bollocks and I've made every word up.

This week, we are at the summit of beauty and love and Venus was her name, she's got it, yeah, baby she's got it, I'm your Venus, I'm your fire at your desire. Sorry, got a bit carried away.

This afternoon you will be having a manicure and haircut before going out to the cinema with that Michael. I know this because I work for the *News of the World* and we've been tapping your phone.

You are almost certainly a woman, a gay man or a rival astrologer from another paper looking for inspiration.

The sun is currently in your third house and he's shagging his girlfriend on your bed.

The stars are lined up with Uranus, now where do you want the rest of the tattoo? Don't worry it will be fine.

Mercury brings out your thoughtful side and an old friend comes to visit today (whilst every effort is made to ensure the accuracy and reliability of Mystic Meg's predictions, this could be complete and utter horse shit).

28 UNLIKELY SALES ADS

It's 3 for the price of 4 week at Carpet Cowboys.

Suck my knob. Offer extended due to unprecedented lack of interest.

If you like pizzas, then perhaps you'd like to give us a call if you're not busy as we are reasonably competent at making them. We have a number of different flavours and are capable of bringing them round to you should you require. Although, if we're being honest, I think by the time you get it, it will probably have gone a bit cold, so on balance you might be better just getting one from the supermarket and heating it up yourself. Thanks for your time.

Shirt for Sale. Really cheap and we're not trying it on.

Do YOU hate housework and ironing? Me, too. Boring or what?

Shit! What a Fucking Brilliant Deal! Look! Don't Miss This You Pricks!

Send your unwanted sheet metal to Cash 4 Tin, in this handy-sized envelope. We pay 50p for every half-ton.

Help! We've massively over-ordered! No one can finish their dinner. Does anyone want half a meat feast pizza and 24 jumbo garlic brickettes?

Exciting New Offer. Today! Won't suck my knob? Then simply tug me off! Hurry! Can't last for ever! (Surely?)

We Steal Any Car … We Steal Any Car …

Worried your breasts are too big? Why not join me for a drink this evening at a lovely little bar I know.

Have you got memory problems? Remember this number and give us a call.

Buy Now! Pay Now!

Iceland Frozen Goods: Our Bank Accounts, Our Assets, Our Tourist Industry.

To mark our hundredth anniversary we've gone back to 1911 prices … and multiplied them by a hundred.

OK! All right! Closing down sale! Just feel it a bit through my trousers!

UNLIKELY VILLAGE NAMES

SULKING-ON-THE-BLOB

Morten Harket
Racist-under-Surface
Little Todger
Ruined-by-Tesco
Sixfingers
Mail-on-Sunday

Upper Bottom
Ant-in-Dec
Lower Hygiene
Fog-on-the-Tyne
Much Fucking
Cheesy End

32 UNLIKELY LINES FROM A SHERLOC

'IT IS A three blow-job problem, Watson,' he said imperiously and I understood, slipping to my knees with a silent nod.

'Bollocks, Watson, I've run out of cocaine, I'll have to do some ketamine.'

'Remember, Watson, eliminate all other factors, and the one which remains, however improbable, must be the truth. So, I conclude that the killer has to be *you* working in conjunction with a carrot called Ian.'

'Holmes, look at these gigantic hound's footprints!'

'Never mind the footprints, Watson, look at the size of the turd you've just knelt in.'

'Foiled, Watson!' said Holmes, thumping his palm with his fist. 'Moriarty has taken out a super-injunction and I can't reveal his crime.'

'Watson, I hear the heavy approach of my brilliant brother, a man who is as omnipotent as he is an omnivore. Please help him through the door and give up all of the sofa to . . . Eamonn Holmes.'

Here, I was going to write of 'The Adventure of the Norwood Builder', but he's said I can't until at least Tuesday when he gets the materials in.

'Moriarty, you are the Napoleon of crime,' Holmes said with a backward glance, 'but luckily for me you are also the Stephen Hawking of diving off the top of a large Swiss waterfall.'

'Watson, these are the Baker Street Irregulars. This group of ragamuffins are my eyes and ears on the streets of London as well as the most lucrative rent boys this side of the Thames. Baker Street apartments don't pay for themselves, you know.'

'Watson, I wish to draw your attention to the curious incident of the dog in the night-time.'
'Nah. Looks shit. I like stuff by John Grisham or Andy McNab.'

'Holmes, you're incredible!' I said. He just winked, rolled off me and, propping himself up on a pillow, lit his meerschaum.

'Dr Bigg-Badman looks guilty to me, Watson.'
'No shit, Sherlock,' I finally got the chance to reply after all these years.

I opened the door on a hideous-looking visage, but then I suppose it is more than thirty years since they had a hit with 'Fade to Grey', so I shouldn't be surprised how much they had aged.

34 UNLIKELY THINGS TO READ O

Another spelling mistake! What the fuck is wrong with you?

It looks like you're downloading illegal porn. Would you like me to not tell the police? How much is it worth?

Christ, this is boring. Can't you go on the Internet for a bit?

Would you like to revert to the saved 'Really Important Work 2011'? Either way you've just lost the document.

Would you like to enable or disable cookies? You can't remember which one you need to do, can you? Either way you're now going to go off and eat a cookie, aren't you? You sad, fat, predictable bastard.

This machine will self-destruct in 21 seconds.

It looks like you are trying to have a wank – would you like me to help?

The computer has updates for your software. Would you like to continue and install now or just have me pop up annoyingly when you're in the middle of something for ever more?

Based on your interests, we have suggested people you might want to befriend on Facebook, and what a sorry fucking shower they are...

I'm sorry but I do not recognize the only printer I'm attached to and the only one I've ever printed on.

Are you sure you want to send this message without a subject as well as that bloody awful picture of you looking like a young Michael Winner?

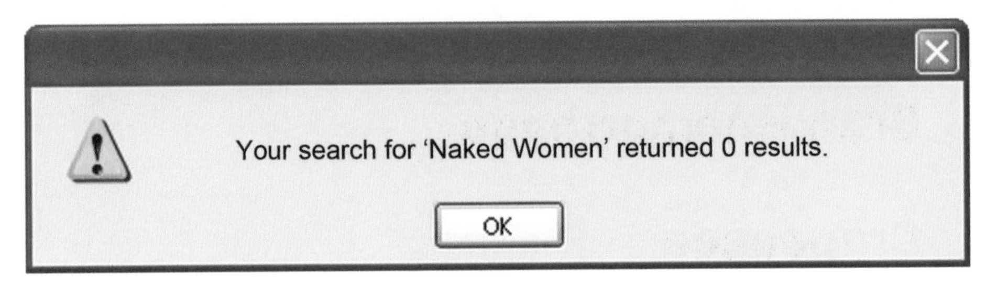

Need a penis reduction?

Hi sexy. I am in London tonight, but I already have a date.

You have 457 Facebook friends. And 2 real ones.

It is now safe to autodelete all your documents.

Looks like you don't know how to turn off your irritating paper clip.

Do you want to autodelete your porn-viewing history?

Are you sure you want to delete this document? Funny how I never seem to say this when you accidentally delete a document you didn't want to lose.

You have pissed away 153 hours of your life playing solitaire.

You have selected erectile-dysfunction.com as your homepage.

36 UNLIKELY NAMES FOR BREAKFAS

Bran Haemorrhage

Crapeesee

Sugar Tits

Frosted Meths

Colonosco Pops

Kellogg's Golden Shower

Psoriasis Flakes

Golden Bollocks

Turd Bullets

NOW
WITH ADDED
VITAMINS
100%
CORN
FLAPS
TASTY & DELICIOUS

38 BAD THINGS TO HEAR AT WOR

'Being an electric chair operator does have its fun side as well.'

'This is really exciting – me, a hospital-prowling weirdo removing an appendix!'

'As you're retiring tomorrow we've put you on the most dangerous case of your career with a brand-new rookie detective.'

'And if any chickens come along the conveyor belt that are still alive ... that's where the mallet comes in.'

'You might want to wear earplugs, it's surprising just how loudly pigs scream.'

'In order to pass the firefighter's initiation you have to slide down everyone's pole.'

'It's always hard stepping into someone else's shoes. Do you mind if we call you Judas?'

'And remember, you wipe the old ladies' bottoms from south to north.'

'Imagine – the club pays eighty million for me and I break my legs on holiday.'

'My wife can't make the shift tonight so I'll be doing the pole dancing for her.'

'Mind if I pull the blinds down? That sunlight's going to keep me awake.'

'My English not so good. When I apply for job I not know what BNP stand for.'

'Wow! At last! Me, the head honcho in the Vatican! Now, where are the girls?'

40 UNLIKELY THINGS TO HEAR O

'Today the Eggheads take on a team from al-Qaeda – hooks on buzzers, please.'

'Hawking, Cambridge. I'm going to have to hurry you.'

'Starter for ten, no conferring – how many of you will end up working at McDonald's despite having a degree?'

'So, Sue, are you nervous? What about if I just gently cup your breast?'

For £32,000...
Is Chris Tarrant:

a) bored;
b) just in it for the money;
c) phoning it in, or
d) all of the above?

TV QUIZ SHOW

'Welcome to ITV's newest quiz show. Question one, draw the molecular structure of DNA.'

'I'm Jeremy Paxman, fingers on noses – HONK!'

'Welcome to *Are You Smarter Than a Ten-Year-Old*? And if you are, why are you watching Sky One on a Saturday evening?'

'Let's have a look at your nine letter word ... ahh, I'm afraid "piss flaps" is two words.'

'A system, Noel? You patronizing tosser, you know perfectly well that opening these boxes is entirely down to chance.'

'What happened next, Sue? Well, I reckon Wayne Rooney shimmied to the left, then put his cock in her mouth.'

'What "S" does it look like I'm having when I wink?'

'Welcome to the *Weakest Link Lloyds Bank Workers Special*. You've banked nothing, scored nothing, but you all get a bonus.'

'Let's have a look at the scores. The teams from Manchester University owe £24,000 and the team from Oxford owe £36,000.'

'And your specialist subject is "Things that have happened to you".'

'So Jesus College Cambridge have 500 points, the four chancers from the University of Life are on minus 10.'

'Yesterday the Eggheads took a battering from the spoons, tonight they take on the soldiers.'

'Welcome to *Quiz Call*. Stop wasting your time – flick over to a porn channel, have a wank and go to bed.'

42 UNLIKELY TITLES FOR MEMOIRS

BILL'O THE BELT: Bill Clinton

LIFE SUCKS: Monica Lewinsky

KILL BILL: Hillary Clinton

BEYOND OUR KEN, THE DIARIES VOLUME 2: Ken Livingstone

IT SHOULDN'T HAPPEN TO A QUEEN: Liz Windsor

THE ART OF LEADERSHIP: Nick Griffin

SOD THE LOT OF YOU: Gordon Brown

LOOK, SHE TOLD ME SHE WAS EIGHTEEN: Roman Polanski

SO, SUDDENLY I'M THE BAD GUY? THE LOST DIARIES OF OSAMA BIN LADEN

IN PRAISE OF YOUNGER WOMEN: Silvio Berlusconi

ASSAD STATE OF AFFAIRS: President Assad of Syria

BALLS DEEP: The Philosophical Enquiries of Ed Balls

KEN LIVINGSTONE

20p

KEN LIVINGSTONE, I PRESUME?

THE DIARIES VOL. 1

44 UNLIKELY THINGS TO HEAR AT A

'Did anyone else hear a muffled screaming and banging as the coffin rolled into the furnace?'

'He wanted this day to be a celebration of his life, but I think all of us who knew him would much rather make it a celebration of his death.'

'Death came for him suddenly that night, well I assume it was Death because he looked like he'd been hacked to bits with a scythe.'

'How did I know Steve? Oh, it was me that killed him.'

'OK, that's him up in flames, let's get that will read!'

'I'm sure you'll agree with me that Michael actually quite suited having no head.'

'It has literally only just occurred to one, that one is now King...'

'Jeff was a special person to so many of us ... sorry, *Keith* was a special person to so many of us.'

'I never knew him in life but he looked fun in the mortuary, so I thought I'd pop along.'

'Bob died as he lived: suffering from an agonizing, incurable wasting disease.'

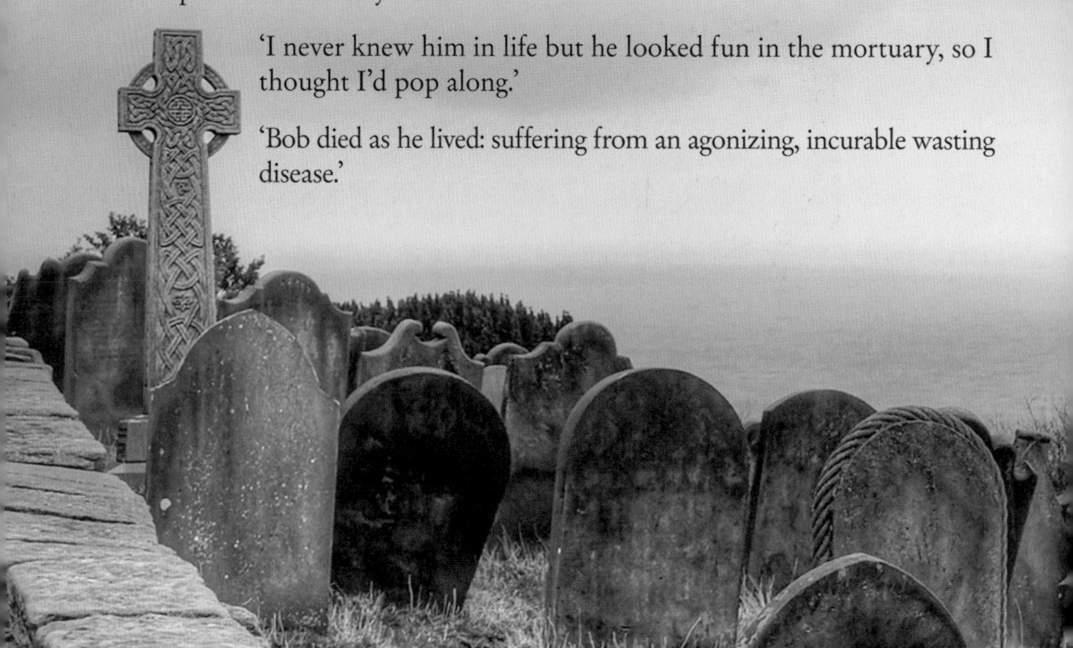

'Why does everyone look so fucking miserable? Come on, people ... let's get this party started!'

'Ladies and gentlemen, make your way to the dance floor and enjoy the music of Mr Marilyn Manson!'

'You're a single woman now and that black dress would look great on my bedroom floor.'

'I'll never forget the last words she said to me ... "Let go ... can't breathe ..."'

'We are all gathered here today, so no one leaves this room until we find out who killed him.'

'I was going to say he'll be looking down on us now, but I think we all know it's going to be rather more of an upward trajectory...'

'It wasn't contagious, was it?'

'Shall I do the bit about him being a loving father, or just cut to the bit about how much you all get?'

'Being a necrophiliac, Bernard has left some very unusual requests for today's ceremony.'

'Let's remember Philip as he would no doubt like to be remembered - dressed in a gimp suit and pounding your wives to the point of hysterical, screeching orgasm.'

'And as we feed Derek's body into this industrial mincer and arrange the tins at the other end, let's all take a moment to muse on just how fond of dogs he was.'

46 UNLIKELY THINGS TO HEAR IN

'Taking steroids will get you muscles the size of melons – and a cock you can fit in a thimble.'

'Starting to feel the burn? That's the friction caused by your huge fat thighs rubbing together.'

'Welcome to this, the first-ever long-toed sloth workout video. And *relax*.'

'Hello, I'm Elle Macpherson and welcome to Wankercise.'

'Right everyone – fag break.'

'Stretch, and stretch, and stretch ... and now you should be able to put those spandex shorts on.'

'It's important not to spend too long on the rowing machine – in case you sink it, you fat pig.'

'This squatting exercise is guaranteed to make you lose pounds – you just take a load of laxatives, and squat over a toilet.'

'Hello, I'm a Roman Catholic priest and you've bought the wrong kind of exorcise video.'

'I'm going to have to stop it there – my pizza's arrived.'

'Warming up is very important – especially with leftover curry.'

'Five a day is what we're aiming for – I still smoke twenty but I'm trying.'

'Welcome to fitness the Ginsters way.'

'To warm up, everyone do three laps round the fat girl on the end.'

'If you want a six-pack – they're two for one at Somerfield.'

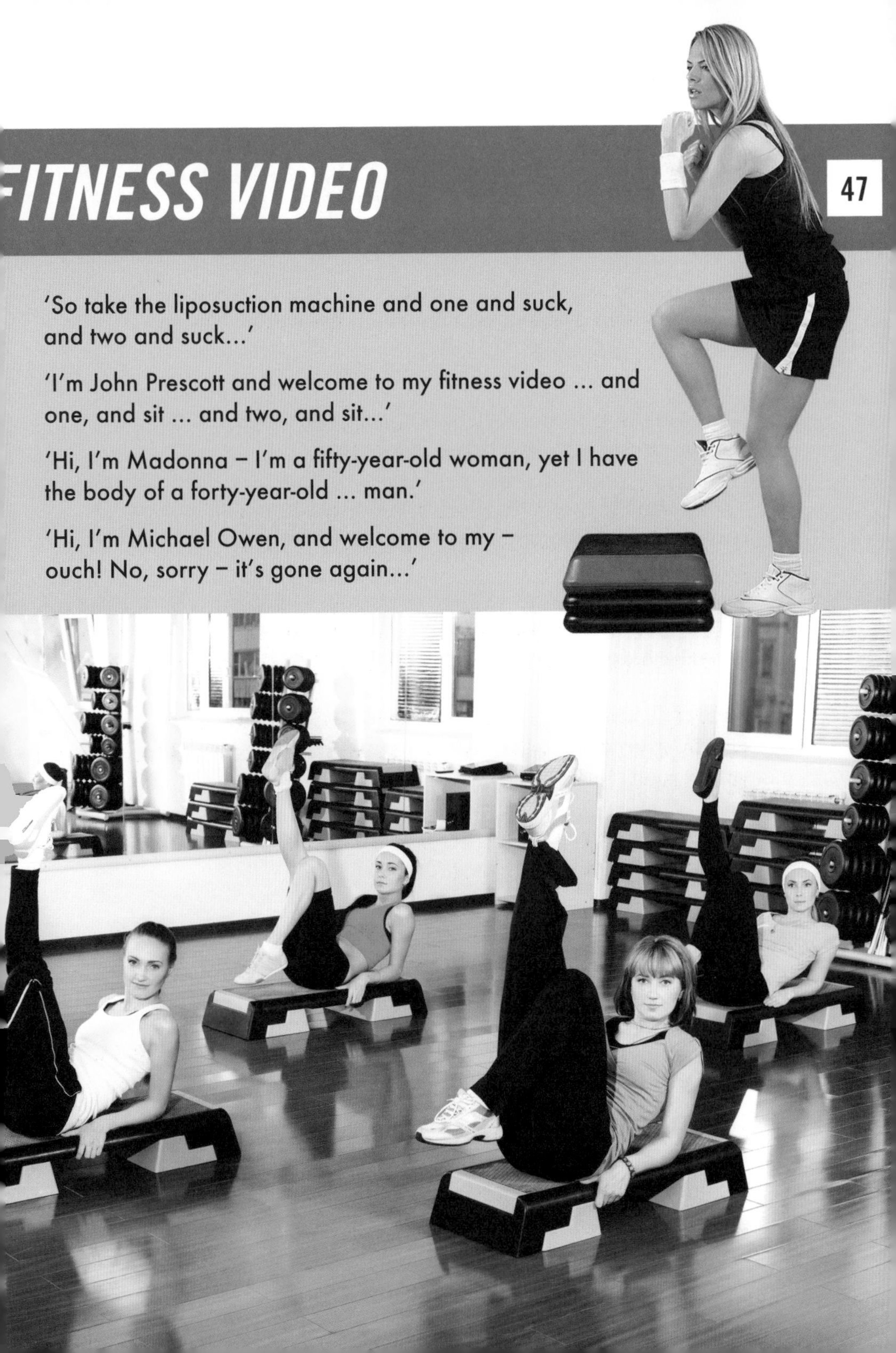

FITNESS VIDEO

'So take the liposuction machine and one and suck, and two and suck...'

'I'm John Prescott and welcome to my fitness video ... and one, and sit ... and two, and sit...'

'Hi, I'm Madonna – I'm a fifty-year-old woman, yet I have the body of a forty-year-old ... man.'

'Hi, I'm Michael Owen, and welcome to my – ouch! No, sorry – it's gone again...'

UNLIKELY THINGS TO READ IN

On no account greet your patient with the words: 'Oh my fucking God! Shit! Arrggghh!'

If the patient begins yawning and gasping for air, you should maybe stop talking and leave them alone.

If the casualty is unconscious and the airway is blocked with a choking hazard, double check you have safely stored away your penis.

Establish trust. Do not make assumptions unless they definitely look like it was their own fault and they should have known better.

A quiet casualty may be unconscious so they should always take priority even if another one is screaming: 'Arrggh! Help! Get this car off me!'

Assess the severity of the casualty's injuries and the risk of cross-infection. If necessary: Finish them.

When approaching the scene of an accident: Stop. Apply the handbrake and turn off your engine. Definitely do it in this order or you might make things worse.

The casualty may look terrible. To help you work at your best try and picture them healthy and ... naked or in lacy underwear.

Elevate patient's leg, and then shout out: 'Has anyone lost this leg?'

If someone at the beach complains of being stung, before urinating on them check they didn't mean by a wasp.

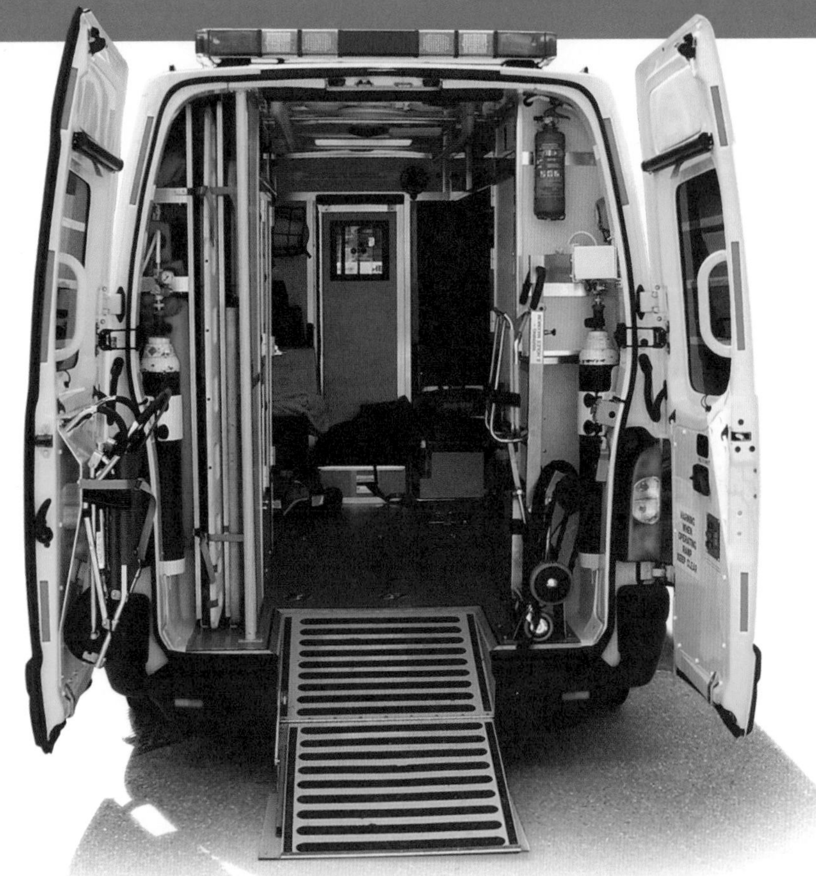

Take care of the casualty's possessions and sort yourself out for your trouble.

If you have sand in your foreskin, try and remove it without looking as though you're having a wank. Equally, if you're having a wank, try and look like you're getting sand out of your foreskin.

If someone's been struck by lightning, comfort them by saying it's unlikely to happen again.

UNLIKELY TUBE STATIONS

Carriage Now Full of
Free Newspapers

I Went Out with a Girl
from Here Once. Dirt.

Nice Kebab Shop Here

Stop Looking
Down That
Girl's Top

Gay Bit

It Smells of
Wee Here

My
Mum's

UNLIKELY HOROSCOPES

Your Stars

By our expert Astrologer

Your life is pointless. Kill yourself.

I predict in exactly ten seconds' time you will say: 'How much do you reckon he gets paid for this shite?'

That new sitcom you were thinking of watching on ITV will be really shit.

Pisces – beware of seemingly delicious worms on metal hooks.

Virgo (titter).

Beware of a tall dark stranger, whose chancellor promises budget cuts.

Beware of a tall dark stranger coming at you with a knife, obviously. You'd be a fool not to.

Think again about that long-distance trip to Delhi you're planning.

Today is a day for big decisions. Why not stop reading this shit?

You could come into a lot of money, but only if you sell Fernando Torres during the transfer window.

Money is not a great worry for you this month as you are a jammy Tory bastard.

Money will be a worry for you. To find out more ring my three-pounds-a-minute helpline.

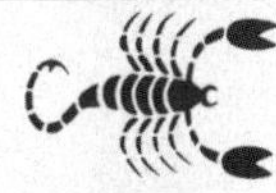

With the sun appearing above your third house, you must be a banker.

Today movements of the planets millions of miles away will have no effect on your life whatsoever.

If it's your birthday today ... I can probably guess your PIN number.

Put your faith in the stars. I've been writing this column now for twenty-two years and it's brought me an astonishingly high average wage.

54 UNLIKELY NAMES FOR NEV

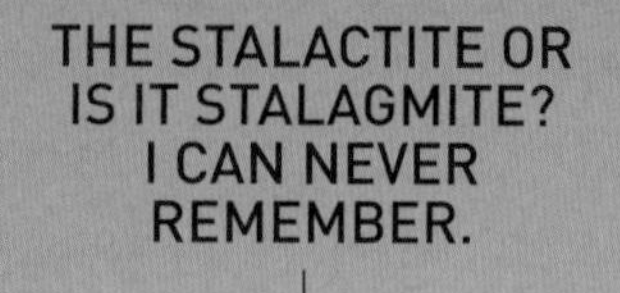

THE STALACTITE OR IS IT STALAGMITE? I CAN NEVER REMEMBER.

THE EJACULATION

THE CHEESE AND HAM CROISSANT WITH LETTUCE AND PICKLE ON THE SIDE

THE TIT

THE HERNIA

THE RONNIE CORBETT

THE HARD O

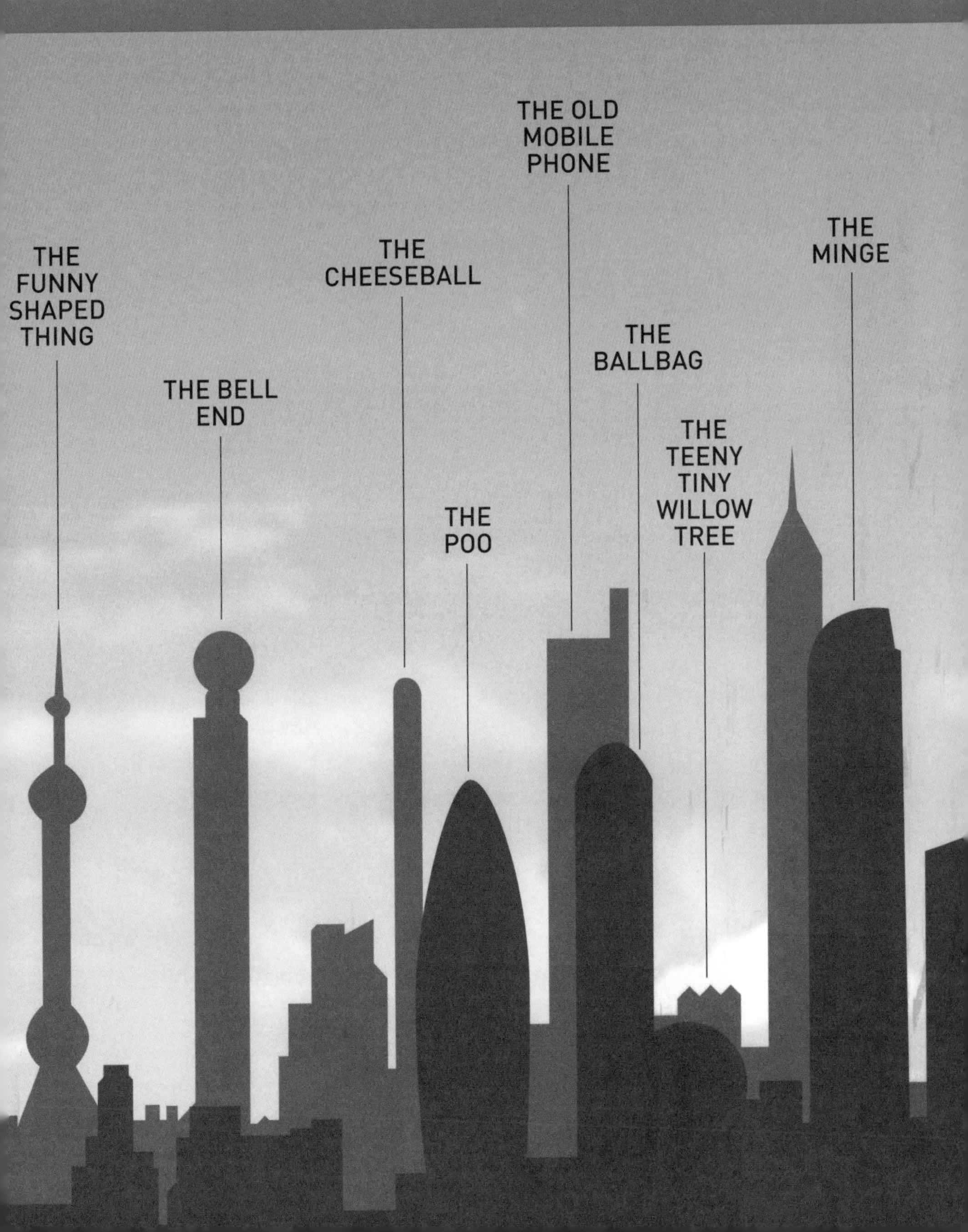
THE FUNNY SHAPED THING
THE BELL END
THE CHEESEBALL
THE POO
THE OLD MOBILE PHONE
THE BALLBAG
THE TEENY TINY WILLOW TREE
THE MINGE

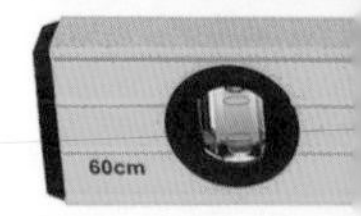

THINGS YOU WOULDN'T HEA

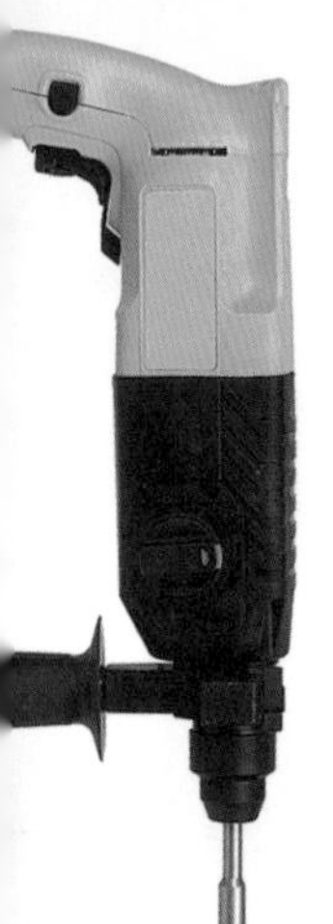

'In just sixty minutes we've totally transformed the feel of your bathroom by letting two of our builders have a poo in it.'

'Failing that, pay for a man to come in and do it properly.'

'And with one tiny tap ... Ronnie Corbett's new bathroom is complete.'

'Next week, bleeding radiators and ... bastard carpets.'

'And here's a room we ruined earlier...'

'Next week's *60 Minute Makeover* will be replaced by a follow-up to this week's episode called *Nine Month Court Case*.'

'While you were out, we got in and have turned your simple sixties bungalow into a squat, free-love centre and art gallery.'

'No, that isn't a water feature, it's just Tommy Walsh having a piss behind the bush.'

'As a surprise while he was working away, Mrs Fritzl asked us to come in and convert the basement to a workshop for her husband, Josef, but we decided it would be much better to do up her loft.'

'Let's show you what Laurence Llewelyn-Bowen has done to your lounge. Hands over your eyes. I mean you, Laurence, she's going to slap you.'

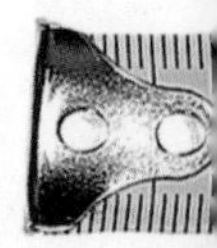

N A DIY SHOW

'Close your eyes and go up to the bedroom, Laurence has something to show you. We'll turn off the cameras.'

'Sixty minutes is all it took for the fumes from the faulty boiler we fitted to kill everyone in the house.'

'You wanted a pond, so we've put one in ... although to be honest it's more of a puddle and it's in your front room.'

'Here's an interesting joint, it's three Rizlas stuffed with Moroccan black.'

'Of course no toolkit is complete without *Nuts* – for builders who are too frightened to buy real pornography.'

'Just have fun with it – there's no rule that says you can only pebble-dash the outside of your house.'

'So what we've done is knock this front room ... well, down really.'

'Now, on the subject of decking – who wants to punch Nick Knowles first?'

'The wall's collapsed and killed everyone!'

'Today we're in Newcastle where we'll be doing some D-Way-Ay.'

58 UNLIKELY RAIL TIMETABLE

0900	Brighton to London
0900	No seats. See how long we can get away with being in First Class
0902	Bastards
0904	Is it too early for a vodka and tonic off the trolley?
0905	No it is not
0906	Get up to go to the loo
0930	Not one working fucking crapper in a twelve coach train
0932	Announcement about not forgetting your belongings
0936	Person opposite kicks you in the shin but you say 'Sorry'
0940	Suitcase falls on old lady
0944	High Court judge shows you his todger
2215	Delay due to waiting for a plausible excuse for delay

1820 London to Manchester
1822 Unscheduled stop
1833 Buffet car runs out of water
1835 Can the guard contact the driver?
1837 That didn't sound good
1838 Can anyone else smell burning?
1839 Don't tell anyone
1840 Milton Keynes Central
1844 Have I got on the wrong one?
1848 Press wrong button, revealing old lady on loo
1850 Girl opposite starts loud mobile conversation
1855 Suitcase falls off overhead shelf but unfortunately misses girl on phone
1902 Delay due to doggers on the line at Stoke

60 UNLIKELY PUZZLES

Solve these anagrams and uncover the common theme:
BLLASAKC-PASSFLIPS-ASERHELO-CUCKSOCKER-MENGI

Use the space below to fill in your bank card PIN number.

Think of a number. Double it. Divide it by 6, add 5, take away the sum of the last two digits of the year you were born, add the age at which you lost your virginity, take away the number of sexual partners, go and have a shit and time how long it takes from first strain to last wipe and then take that number away, saw through one of your toes . . . (cont. p.456)

Mrs Tiggywinkle has gone to the shops, got lost and can't find her way home. Do us a favour, could you get in the car and go and pick her up?

Match these serial killers to their victim!

If a football game lasts ninety minutes and no one has been injured, calculate how much injury time will be played if Manchester United are not winning.

Match the stool sample to the foodstuff.

Idi Amin is torturing and killing an opponent. Join the dots to find out which body part he is about to break off and eat!

Match these men's faces to their knobs.

Work out which of these three little pigs will be blown to bits by which of the rusting, volatile World War II mines

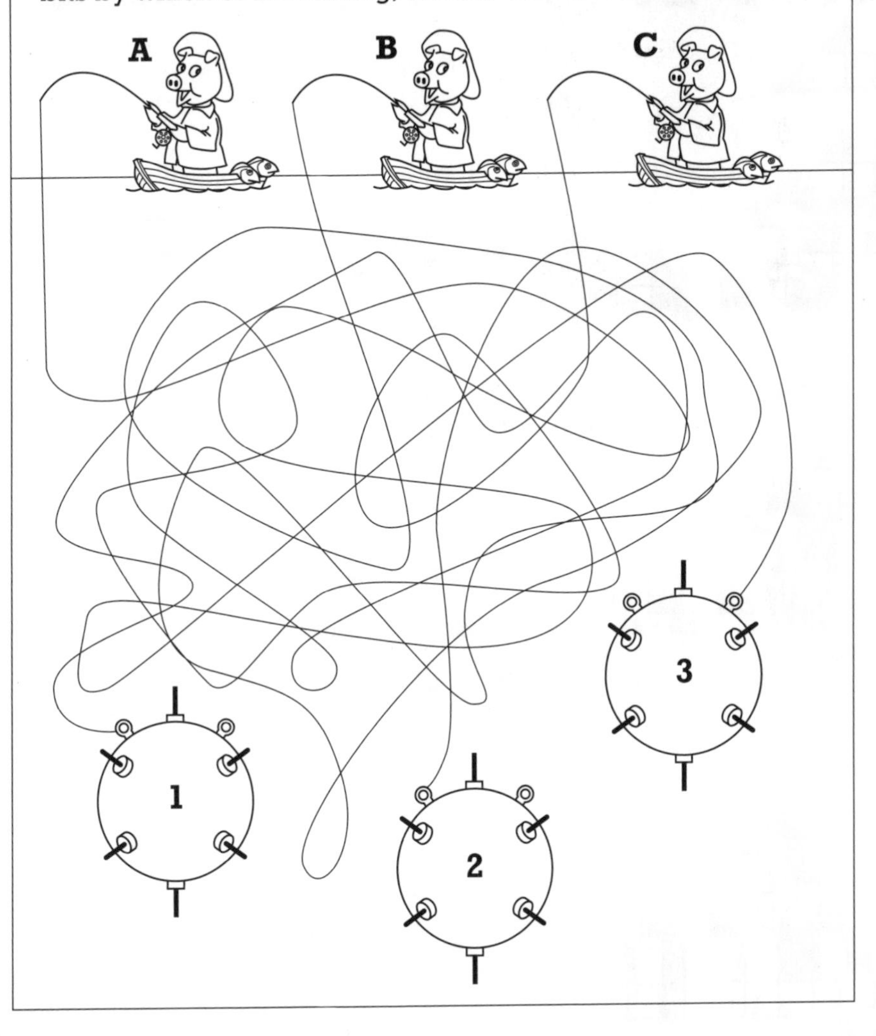

62 UNLIKELY LINES FROM A SHERLOC

IT HAD BEEN a singularly exacting day. Holmes lit his pipe, let the fumes overcome him and flopped back onto the beanbag as the music climbed in volume to match his hallucinations.

'Whatever are you going to do, Holmes?' I asked, wondering whether to leave the room. Silently, he unzipped his trousers and reached a bony hand inside to bring out his rod-like member.

Holmes sat with his eyes tightly closed and his thin nose thrust forward like a beak. 'Don't speak to me for at least fifty minutes while I think this out,' he growled.

'Inspector Lestrade!' shouted Holmes as the tall policeman strode into our rooms at breakfast. 'I have solved the riddle of the four mysterious figures on the Admiral's wall...'

'Fuck that, Mr Holmes!' said the inspector. 'We've got another dead prozzy in Whitechapel, now get your arse in gear.'

'This is a case for Mr Sherlock Holmes if I'm not very much mistaken.'

'Yes. Just leave it on the table, thanks.'

'Mr Holmes, you will have heard, of course, of the Hound of the Baskervilles...' Sir Charles said, his face ashen with fear. Holmes nodded and Sir Charles spoke on, 'Well, the stupid bastard has only gone and mauled a toddler!'

It was quite a sight that greeted me that morning. Holmes, as ever, was sat in his favourite chair, his bony knees jutting out towards a smaller, younger figure knelt on the floor. They were poring over an array of papers strewn across the floor, each dense with text and indecipherable symbols. 'Leave us, Watson, I am in the process of upgrading my mobile phone. This is Dwayne from the shop.'

'This is indeed a terrible thing,' Holmes sulked. 'Guy Ritchie and Robert Downey Jr? I thought Leonard Nimoy was bad enough.'

'Watson, the game's afoot!' Holmes ejaculated. Once more I pretended not to notice a detail you will remember from our earlier case, 'The Dodgy Stain on the Trousers'.

'I fear the count was not being entirely honest with us about the health of his marriage to Countess von Schmidt, Watson.'
'Incredible. How can you tell, Holmes?'
'He sucked me off on Hampstead Heath last Tuesday night.'

'What takes your fancy today, Holmes?' I asked. 'Morphine or cocaine?'
'Neither, my dear Watson. This shit is called "miaow miaow". You want some, Blud?'

64 UNLIKELY SALES ADS

AVAILABLE! Chemical weapons. EVERYTHING MUST GO! Contact err … Mike … Badaffi … Libya (yes, that's my real name).

Crazy Prices! They're mad! This £10.99 bottle of wine, NOW £600! These 59p packet of crisps now £430! It's crazy! And that's not all … we're selling these glasses that wouldn't fetch 30p at a car boot sale for £67 each! Don't Miss Out!

For Sale: Sign

1992 Austin Princess – 2p or nearest offer

Lose Weight in three weeks with the new 'Shit Yourself Diet'. Get your Part Warmed Chicken and Dodgy Egg Cookbook now.

Is your skin saggy? Me too. Bummer, isn't it?

Chips! Chips! Chips! Chips! Guess what I sell? That's right. Wood.

Exciting New Offer. Today! Won't suck my knob? Then simply tug me off! Hurry! Can't last for ever! (Surely?)

Learn basic etiquette – and don't come into my fucking shop again before you do.

Massive Cockroach Infestation. Hurry. Buyer Collects.

Human Organs. We Sell and BUY. Great rates. Removal and transplant FREE to customers who quote this ad.

We're literally giving this stuff away which is why we're literally going out of business.

It's Mad Marriage Month at People Traffickers. Eastern European women now at low, low, low prices. Come on down.

MATTRESSES! BATHS! MOTORCYCLE PARTS! They're all piled in my garden. Help yourself.

Can you tell the difference between top of the range moisturizer and cheap foreign imitations? No? Brilliant. Come to my shop now.

Learn how to avoid being swindled or your money back.

We've Gone Crazy Here at the Chair Warehouse! We've shot fourteen customers and are about to turn our guns on ourselves.

We'll treat your erectile dysfunction problems with the dignity and decorum they deserve. Contact us at Floppywilly.com

We've Messed Up. We've Massively Over Ordered. Come and view millions of Orange Leather Footrests being shoved up our Head of Supply's rectum. Daily.

66 BAD THINGS TO SAY TO

'Officer, have you got the time? Because I've got the erection.'

'Would you like me to shoot you in the face and send you back to the 1980s?'

'I demand my phone call – I'm going to call a premium-rate sex line for two hours.'

'Of course I was driving erratically, have you any idea how much I've had to drink?'

'Do you mind if I touch your horse ... with my penis?'

'I feel so much safer on this protest with you and your colleagues around.'

'Excuse me, officer, do you know where I can buy some peroxide, garden fertilizer, a small alarm clock and a rucksack? Is it near a tube station?'

'Don't just stand there looking, officer – get in the back seat and join in.'

POLICEMAN

'I much preferred it when you lady police wore skirts, not trousers.'

'I do not recognize your Earth laws.'

'You serve the public, I'm the public, now do as you're told and fuck off.'

'Yes, sorry, I did dial 999 ... I'm always getting you lot and Domino's mixed up.'

'Are you here for the dogging?'

'Hey blud, you is on the wrong territory, man.'

'If you're filming this for *Traffic Cops* then I want regular Equity rate plus repeat fees and image rights.'

'I was just Tweeting about how well you were doing to keep up with me.'

'Why don't you give me a sample of *your* DNA, big boy?'

'No this isn't an actual riot, officer, we're the Student Protests Re-enactment Society.'

68 UNLIKELY THINGS TO HEAR IN

'OK roll up, roll up for this afternoon's show. Mums and dads: feel free to have a bet with Bruno our bookmaker as we present ... Grizzly versus Polar – to the death!'

'Look Dad, you can see him having a poo!'
'Oi, close the toilet door you little bastard!'

'Wow! I just saw something move in one of those reptile tanks!'

'But why are we here, Dad? You're not even divorced.'

'Whose idea was it to put Mouse World next to the python enclosure?'

'Actually, son, that panda did get punched in the eye twice.'

'We at Nature Park take our responsibility to the natural world very seriously. But now roll up to see Fifi the juggling tiger ride her unicycle through the hoop of fire.'

'The rare African mole is one of nature's best diggers, as you can see by the empty enclosure.'

'Daddy, why's that monkey not wanking?'

'Some of our animals of course are sponsored by celebrities. That giant beaver was donated by Graham Norton.'

'I'm afraid the chimpanzees aren't here today. They were double booked with their piano-removal business.'

'Please do not feed the animals. Human food reacts badly with the massive doses of illegal tranquilizer we've put them on.'

'Yes, it's 1 p.m. and to spice things up, we're letting the tigers out.'

ZOO

'They share 97% of our DNA and in some cases can be taught to play up front for Manchester United and England.'

'Put down your car aerial or the monkeys will repeatedly pull on it. Instead, why not leave your window open and your flies undone?'

'OK, nobody move. Nobody fucking move ... keep your eyes fixed on him and start to back very slowly away...'

'The last time I saw an arse that red was at your uncle's stag weekend.'

'If you enjoyed the elephant show, there's a range of ivory goods in the gift shop.'

'Come over here, Son – look at the size of its cock!'

'And a big round of applause for Jenny as she slips down Shamu the Killer Whale's throat.'

70 UNLIKELY ELEMENTS

1	2	3	4
1 AD Adnauseum	Atomic # Symbol Name		
2 B Berlusconium	5 G My big fat gypsum		
3 DTT Donttouchthis-whateveryoudo	6 R Rohypnol		
4 FA Fandabbee-dozium	7 F Fuckonium	8 SH Shit	9 SP Spunk

Solid

Liquid

Gas

Unknown

5	6	7	
			1
	13 AU Auditorium	14 TR Trumpton	2
			3
0 SN not	11 O Oxygène by Jean Michel Jarre	12 US Uselessium	4

BAD WAYS TO START A SPEECH

'Friends, Romans, C*nt ... sorry my autocue just stuck.'

'OK let's riff!'

'Give me an H! Give me an E! Give me an L!'

'Only about fifty times before in the field of human conflict has so much been owed by so many to so few.'

'I had a dream, but then I woke up and I couldn't remember it. Have you ever done that? There was a dog in it, I think.'

'Life's not been easy since I was diagnosed a homicidal psychopath.'

'This has been a highly successful year for the school since we don't let the thick kids in any more.'

'To make this easier for me, I'm going to imagine you all naked. To make it easier for you, I am naked.'

'Listen up, you slags.'

'Mr Speaker, I plan to deliver this year's budget speech in mime.'

'We will fight them on the beaches, and if we don't win in half an hour, we'll surrender.'

'Good afternoon, Dagos!'

'Before you take to the dance floor, we are obliged to give you a health and safety briefing: don't shag Jenny in Accounts.'

'In summing up, ladies and gentlemen, my client is guilty; no, innocent, hang on, which side am I on?'

'It's always difficult to speak at a funeral, especially when it was you who ran over the deceased.'

'My God, but you're an ugly looking bunch.'

'Let me start by telling you the one about the bridegroom and the Thai prostitute.'

'Ladies, gentlemen, my slut of an ex-wife...'

'Hang on, before you judge me, let me explain why I've blacked up.'

'Terrorists have seized the building! Now that I've got your attention...'

'Good evening and *Sieg Heil*!'

74 UNLIKELY SUPERHEROES

THE SPERM
MILD SURPRISE MAN
THE GREAT SOPRENDO
CAPTAIN BIRDSEYE
JOHN O'SHEA
PRINCESS MICHAEL
HEDGEHOG
CAPTAIN SOMALIA
ANNETTE
CAPTAIN PAEDO
THE BEVERLEY SISTERS
SPIDERY-WRITING MAN
MONDEO MAN
THE ROHYPNOL KID
CAPTAIN LATTÉ
ENFANT TERRIBLE
WUNDERKIND

BITCHY TEXT MAN

76 UNLIKELY TV LISTINGS

TV Listings

09.00 Come Dine With One Big Fat Gypsy Every Minute
Channel 4 consolidate all their most recent hits into one show in an attempt to make up for the loss of *Big Brother*.

09.30 Downton Abbeys
Former Middlesex and England wicket-keeper Paul Downton visits some of his favourite large religious buildings. This week: Bath.

10.30 Tory Shore
More fun with the housemates in their big blue Bournemouth summer share. Cleggi boasts about his conquests in front of Sam Cam and Theresa May whilst 'the Cable Guy' takes a grenade for Dave 'the Big Society' Cameron.

11.00 Vet Inaction
Newly qualified equine inseminator Peter sits around in his pants doing bugger all and watching TV.

11.30 Mild at Heart
With the court case over the access road looming, Danny goes all out to save the hedgehogs, meanwhile Du Plessis and Alice rescue a tabby from a tree in someone's garden.

12.30 How the World Began
Professor Brian Cox and Dr Alice Roberts illustrate the origins of the human race by ripping off each other's fig leaves and going at it like it's just been invented. It's what the nation wants.

1.30 Take Me Out
Facing the girls this week: Julian Assange, Jason Manford, Silvio Berlusconi and John Terry.

2.30 The Only Way is Essex
A documentary looking back at Essex's 1979 County Championship-winning side. This week: Captain Keith Fletcher is faced with a bowling crisis after injuries to spinners Ray East and David Acfield. Luckily Graham Gooch and John Lever are on top form in a match with Leicestershire at Grace Road.

3.15 Countryfile
A walk through the Malvern Hills, a ride on the Blaenau Ffestiniog railway and the weather for the week ahead. Not as dull as it sounds though because we've got rid of all the wrinkly old birds and it's just wall-to-wall totty.

4.00 The Sunday Night Show
Adrian Chiles presents *The One Show* on ITV but makes it different by saying 'shit' and 'fuck' and showing a picture of some tits.

8.30 Celebrity Masturbate
Tonight's semi-finalists in the big, black, rubber-covered chair are Robson Green picturing fish, Vanessa Feltz imagining bathing in chocolate and cream, Chris Tarrant thinking about middle-aged blondes and Piers Morgan frenziedly shouting out his own name.

9.00 Cowboy Builders
Investigating a poorly finished extension that has gone over budget. Dom Littlewood is killed in a shootout by 'Wild Jim' Johnson and 'The Topeka Kid'.

9.30 Escape to the Country
Raoul Moat presents (repeat).

10.00 A History of the World in Two Objects
Martin Jarvis sits in a chair with a laptop and reads out a downloaded Wikipedia entry. This week: The Romans.

11.00 The Only Way is Wigan
Doreen and Shane fall out when her fake tan runs whilst watching an amateur rugby league match in the rain. Shaun is beaten up by bouncers on King Street and Mary meets resistance in her attempts to vajazzle a pie in Greggs.

11.30 Ice Road Traffic Wardens
Bobo amazes an Inuit van driver by sledging out to the slopes of Atigun Pass and giving him a ticket for being slightly over his bay markings.

12.00 Jukebox Jewry
Host Simon Amstell is joined by Matt Lucas, Claudia Winkleman and Benjamin Netanyahu to run the rule over the new entries in the hit parade.

00.30 Britain's Next Top Homosexual
Wannabe singers, TV presenters and politicians compete in front of a panel of John Barrowman, Cilla Black and Wayne Sleep for the chance to become BFFs with Sir Elton John.

01.30 Film: Yentob (1983)
Romantic musical drama starring Barbra Streisand as a young Polish girl who wears a fake beard and sun tan to pass herself off as a TV executive who only makes documentaries starring herself. Topol co-stars as Mark Thompson.

04.00 A History of British C*nts
Piers Morgan presents a comprehensive twelve-part journey through the biggest wankers in our country's long history. This week: Hengist, Horsa and Ethelred the Unready.

78 BAD THINGS TO HEAR IN HOSPITAL

'You wanted a sex-mad nurse who offered hand relief? My name's Derek.'

'There's a reason you can't feel your legs – we've cut your arms off.'

'You wanted a penis *enlargement*? Oh dear. Well, at least now anything we do is going to look better than that.'

'OK, this monitor shows your heart – and when this light flashes you need to put another £2 coin in the meter. You'll need about forty quid to get you through the night.'

'It was your left leg? Was that *my* left, or *your* left?'

'Actually nurse, I *did* mean boil his prick.'

'Let me explain what's going to happen. This small umbrella is going to go up your penis. Because some sod has taken the umbrella stand.'

'Congratulations, Miss Jones – you're pregnant! We all had a go on you while you were having your tonsils out.'

'Nurse – the screens! Now these are the slides from my holiday...'

'We've had your HIV test back and I'm pleased to say the results are extremely positive.'

'We have had to cut our cleaning budget, but don't worry – once a week we let the people from the obsessive-compulsive ward come round with a mop.'

'It's a buoy! Now tell me again, how did it get up your arse?'

'Ignore the camera crew, they're
here all week from ITV's *Cowboy Doctors from Hell* series.'

'I'm the Doctor, and these are the Medics. In a minute, you'll be going on up to the *Spirit in the Sky*.'

'It's twins! Now how many other Schwarzenegger DVDs have you got up there?'

80 UNLIKELY FAIRGROUND RIDES

DOWNTON ABBEY – THE RIDE
THROUGH THE ARSEHOLE
THE TUNNEL OF CHEESE
PUSHED OFF A CLIFF
THE REALLY-NOT-SAFE-A-COASTER
RUNAWAY TOYOTA
THE BIKE & SMALL HILL
RUNNING WITH DWARVES
HEALTH & SAFETY NIGHTMARE
THE SHIT YOURSELF
THE PETER SUTCLIFFE GHOST TRAIN
THE SALMONELLA EXPERIENCE
NOT WORTH THE QUEUE
THE C*NT OF LOVE
WHEEL OF VOMIT
THE BIG PINK COCK
THE LITTLE SLIDE

STUCK AT THE TOP

82 UNLIKELY TITLES FOR MEMOIRS

MY TOUGH LIFE SO FAR: David Cameron

I MAY HAVE BEEN IN THE HITLER YOUTH, BUT AT LEAST I'M NOT A PAEDOPHILE: Pope Benedict XVI

MY STRUGGLE (WITH THE ALPHABET): Kerry Katona

LOOK GOOD MY WAY: John McCririck

FOR WHOM THE BELL TOLLS: The Musings of Ian Bell

BECOMING A FOOTBALL LEGEND DESPITE MY DYSLEXIA: Daveham Beckid

DULL TO READ IT, TO READ IT, DULL: Bruce Forsyth

LET'S SEE HOW HE BLOODY LIKES IT - THE UNOFFICIAL JULIAN ASSANGE STORY

ME IN 100 WORDS: Fabio Capello

IT'S GONNA COST YOU, LUV - THE PRINCE ANDREW STORY

STUFF I'VE SHOVED UP MY NOSE AND OTHER TALES: Charlie Sheen

BRIDGE OVER THE RIVER KWAI: The Collected Travel Writings of Wayne Bridge

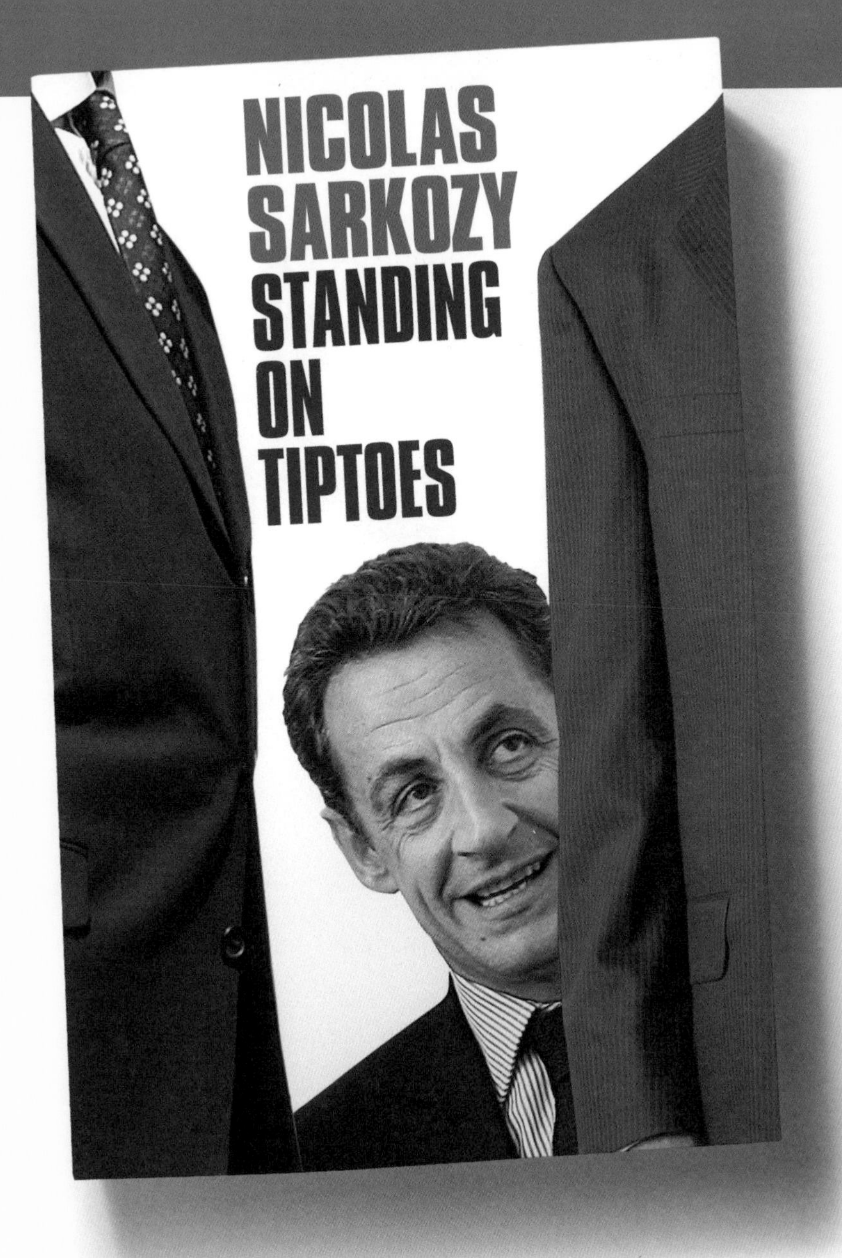
NICOLAS
SARKOZY
STANDING
ON
TIPTOES

84 THINGS YOU WON'T READ IN TH

'I know you turned the water into wine, Jesus, but I didn't have a starter so I should still pay less.'

And Noah did throw his hands up in despair and say, 'Where am I going to get a fucking *narwhal*?'

If a man doth commit adultery with the wife of a neighbour, this is known as 'Shitting on Your Own Doorstep'.

And David looked at Goliath and said, 'Fuck that, he's massive!' and ran off.

And there was no room at the inn, despite Lenny Henry promising two nights for £29.99.

After curing the lame, Jesus saw a burning bush and said, 'You want to put a bit of yoghurt on that.'

And on the fifth day, God was still waiting for a skip.

And on the sixth day, God put a bunch of dinosaur skeletons in the ground, saying, 'That'll confuse 'em.'

'Oh, nothing,' said Eve as she beheld Adam for the first time. 'I just thought it would be bigger.'

'I'm cured!' said the leper, laughing his head off.

'And lo in the land of milk and honey we will get some chocolate, and we can make Toblerone.'

And Moses came down with the Commandments and said, 'I have bad news for Steve, the oxen coveter.'

And Joseph said, ''Tis a colourful coat and will one day make a fine musical.'

When a woman is having her monthly sickness, do not uncover her nakedness. Best just to get her some chocolates, flowers and a DVD and piss off out of her way.

And the room was crowded with Philistines watching Samson and he did shout, 'This is art, you wankers. I'm wasting my time here!' and flounced off in the middle of 'Over the Rainbow'.

If a man takes his wife and her mother also, then this is called a 'Sportsman's Double' and is verily mighty impressive.

'Where is my brother's keeper?' said Jesus. 'The monkeys have escaped again.'

'Oh go on, Eve,' said Adam. 'It's not going to suck itself.'

UNLIKELY THINGS TO HEAR IN

'I hope you don't think I'm easy. I'll have a Rohypnol and tonic, please.'

'It's Jedward night, so please welcome tonight's first Jedward tribute act...'

'Do you know what would look good on my bedroom floor – you. No, your dress... your pants, something – look, will you give us a shag?'

'I seem to be monopolizing your friend, why don't I bring over my fat mate to talk to you?'

'Excuse me, darling, I tucked twenty pounds into your pants about ten minutes ago, and I'm still waiting for my change.'

'I haven't had this much fun clubbing since I went seal-hunting in Alaska.'

'Sorry, I haven't any cash for this lap dance, can I swipe my credit card between your arse cheeks?'

'I've just seen that girl you're with having a slash at the urinals!'

'There you go, mate, £20 a gram – that is pure, uncut, Grade A Shake

'It's Friday night, it's almost midnight and you're in Chorley's number one venue...'

'Mr Stringfellow has sent these drinks over with his compliments, madam.'

'If I said you had a beautiful body, would you let me take you up the arse?'

'It's 80s night! You can only come in with a Filofax, mullet or Rubik's cube. Half price entry for the unemployed, HIV positive or Conservative.'

'Welcome to the VIP area and yes that is Ray Stubbs and Keith Chegwin. Don't stare.'

'Four superstar DJs for you tonight: Ken Bruce, Alan Titchmarsh, Dave Lee Travis and Ed 'Stewpot' Stewart.'

'This is the chillout area, or "outside" as we call it.'

'I asked for a slow comfortable screw, not to be taken roughly up

UNLIKELY THINGS TO READ IN A

INSTRUCTIONS

- Shut up. Sit Down. Fuck Off.
- Step four: realize that there is a screw missing and it is too late to go back.
- Lower trousers and underpants. Position posterior over bowl. Eject faecal matter into Area 3 as shown. Read the paper. Have a fag. Go back to work.
- Press button saying 'menu'. Wait five seconds then start angrily pressing every button on the remote.
- Yup, it is as complicated as it looks. Good luck.
- Follow the diagram, trying not to get distracted by the fact we have made the woman so sexy compared to the man.
- 1. Agree peace in our time.
  2. Annexe Sudetenland.
  3. Invade Poland.
  4. Enjoy your Second World War.
- Step 377. Realize you've done it wrong and dismantle.
- Instructions for using this sandwich toaster: week one, eat nothing but toasted sandwiches; week two, put in back of cupboard and never use again.
- No. Don't do that, mate. Oh God.

NSTRUCTION MANUAL

1. Grasp handle firmly with both hands and pull sword from stone.

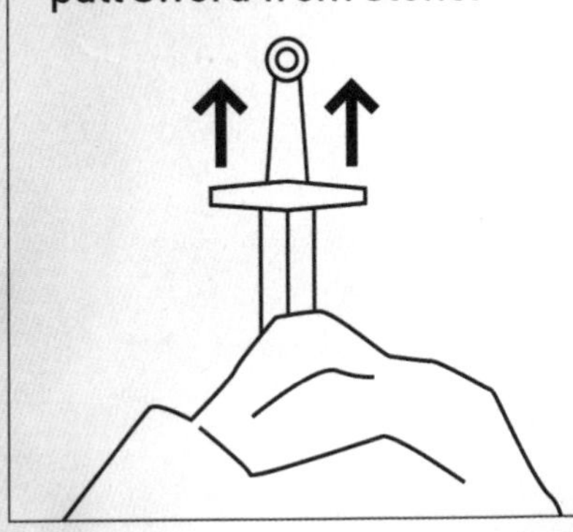

2. Declare self rightful king and heir of Uther Pendragon.

3. Lob sword in lake.

UNLIKELY THINGS TO HEAR O

'Welcome to *Countdown* – yes, it's just weeks until you die.'

'And now our new property series – *A Place in the Rain* – where a Spanish family moves to Wales.'

'Here's today's Conundrum: E M P L O Y E D U N.'

'And now the news where you live – dinner's going to be late, and it's your turn to give Charlie a bath.'

'Welcome to *Deal or No Deal*. It's Box 14. There. That's saved you an hour, now go and do something useful with your life.'

'Well, that's certainly a discovery in your attic, we should probably call a coroner.'

'And now the next in our series of films, entitled *Too Crap for Evening Television*.'

'Welcome to this special edition of Jeremy Kyle – "My Boyfriend Disagrees with My Interpretation of Nietzsche".'

'And you can see *Doctors* shortly, but first it's *Doctors' Receptionists*.'

'Next up is *Teletubbies Uncut* – where we get to see Tinky Winky's winky, and Dipsy's la-la.'

'And now our exciting new daytime quiz entitled *Who Wants to Win a Couple of Hundred Quid*? Ready to play. This question for 75p…'

'Now for our special programme for asylum seekers – *Escape to This Country*.'

'Next up – *Holmes Under the Hammer*. Eamonn Holmes comes face to face with the Yorkshire ripper.'

'Today's *Diagnosis Murder* has been replaced by *Lesbian Nurses Lovefest II*.'

'Coming up next, *Loose Women*, and today's subject … doesn't really matter, they'll just be talking shite anyway.'

AYTIME TV

'Next up the Chuckle Brothers go tea-bagging and tromboning.'

'Now *Friends* – The One You Haven't Seen Before.'

'Then it's *Cash in the Attic*, where a family discover the former Wimbledon champion, Pat Cash, living in their attic.'

'Replacing those gardening sleuths Rosemary and Thyme are those three detectives based at a waxing clinic – Back, Sack and Crack.'

THINGS YOU WON'T HEAR O

'Now in the film there the victim was very attractive, but in reality she was a bit of a moose, wasn't she?'

'Don't have nightmares. No, don't fall asleep, because that's when they'll come for you!'

'Were you there? Did you see anyone acting "a bit foreign"?'

'I'm not saying it's been a quiet month, but our first reconstruction is a Hertfordshire gang terrorizing their estate by knocking on doors and running away.'

'When I said to call if you saw anything at all, I clearly did not fucking want: "A floating plastic bag swirling, buffeted by the strong September wind, danced around by a chorus line of russet leaves".'

'Well, we've employed a psychological profiler and they've told us the killer is almost certainly a bad person who probably has no qualms about breaking the law.'

'We've had one very good lead and police are on their way there now, so if you did it, I'd scarper while there's still time.'

'Please dial if you have any information about this phone scam and remember, even if you can't get through you may still be charged for your call at our standard rate.'

'In our "Rogue's Gallery" this month: Barry Jones is a 46-year-old sex offender from Wakefield and he's done this lovely riverbank watercolour.'

'Having studied dental records, police are confident the man they are looking for has a cavity in his right upper molar.'

'The victim has given police a description of the man: he is 35 to 45, handsome, GSOH. He enjoys reading, travel and following lone women at night.

'We've had twenty-five calls all giving us the same name – Keyser Söze.'

94 UNLIKELY ELEMENTS

Key:

- Solid
- Liquid
- Gas
- Unknown

	9	10	11
1			
2		16 K Klingon	17 SX Spandex
3		22 SC Scrotum	23 DK Dikadumdu
4	28 RS Ray Stubbs	29 Zz Noonereadsthisfar- downthetableium	

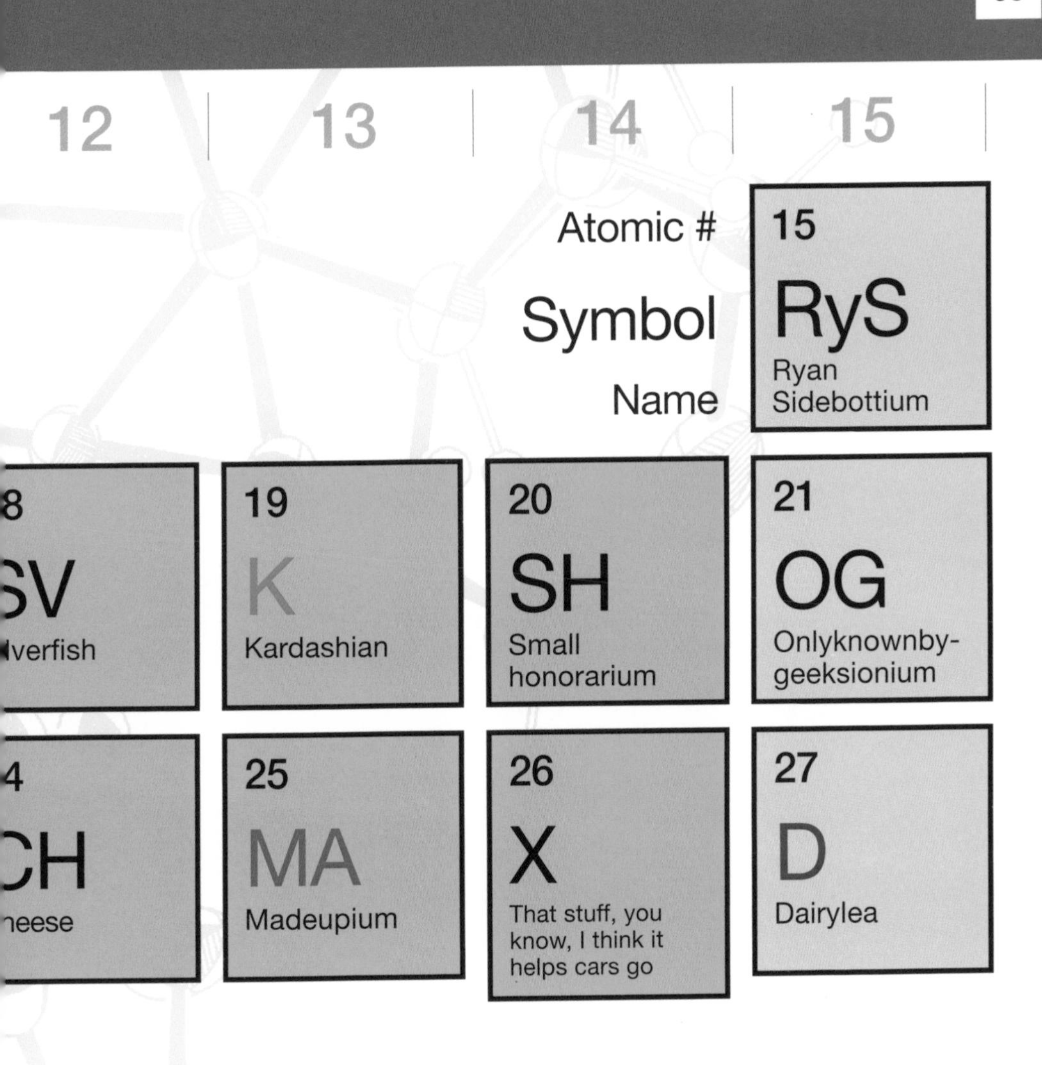
12
13
14
15
Atomic #
Symbol
Name
15
RyS
Ryan Sidebottium
19
K
Kardashian
20
SH
Small honorarium
21
OG
Onlyknownby-geeksionium
25
MA
Madeupium
26
X
That stuff, you know, I think it helps cars go
27
D
Dairylea

UNLIKELY INDEX

Index

98 UNLIKELY NAMES FOR BREAKFAS

Shit Bulker

Corn Piles

Kellogg's Crunchy Klingons

Beefybix

Indeterminate Sludge

Mackerel Puffs

Shredded Paper

Whisky Pops

Porridge Scott and Oates

Wheatashit

Tasty and nutritious
Fucked
Wheat

Chapter 7

'Sir, 006 wants to come in from the cold, he says his cock is about to drop off.'

'I know you were under pressure, Bond, but you wiped out an entire Afghan wedding.'

The bellhop's palm closed around the note as he backed self-consciously out of the door. Bond was now alone in his suite. His cruel, cold eyes began their routine surveillance of the wicker chairs, the marble bathroom and the vast bed. It was time for the secret agent to begin his hotel arrival ritual: he stripped naked and padded into the bathroom for a wank.

'For your next mission, Bond, take off all your clothes and zip yourself up in this hold-all.'

'All the great men are maniacs, Mr Bond,' mused Dr No. 'The great scientists, the religious leaders … Robbie Savage.'

'Here's your car, Bond. Four fenders, seats are a feather bed. Sleek as a thoroughbred. Chitty Chitty Bang Bang, we call it. Apparently the author's become a bit fucking obsessed.'

'The situation is serious, Bond: England has been brought to the brink of ruin by the evil Mr Capello.'

'Yes, Bond, there have been one or two budget cuts, but here's your latest gadget – it's a combined egg-cutter and potato peeler.'

With swift, almost imperceptible movements he fired twice – CLICK CLICK – and prepared to reload. Bond's dexterity impressed M. 007 was plainly one of the department's most effective employees. No one could staple paperwork as efficiently as him.

102 UNLIKELY THINGS TO HEAR FRO

'Give us a minute, just finishing these crisps.'

'You're watching Men and Motors – in the hope of seeing a little bit of tit.'

'You're watching BBC Four. Probably by accident. Have you fallen asleep? Wakey wakey!'

'If you've been affected by any of the issues raised in tonight's programme then don't bother writing to us because we genuinely don't give a fuck about you.'

'She's fat, she's back – it's Fern Britton.'

'Stay tuned for the News – and I've been assured by Huw Edwards that tonight's is a cracker.'

'You're watching Living TV, you sad, pointless fuck.'

'And now on BBC One, something that looks like a Hungarian sitcom from 1982 dubbed over by Irish people ... *Mrs Brown's Boys.*'

'Gok Wan up next, but enough about what I'm doing ... here's *Hollyoaks.*'

'And now on Channel 4 a sympathetic exploration of traveller culture in *Ha! Look at the Pikeys!*'

'Coming up, a cutting-edge special about that big murder in the news put together so quickly that we must have reacted before the police.'

'And now live coverage of the big FA Cup quarter-final tie. Shit on the City doo dah...'

'If you love comedy then later on tonight I wouldn't bother watching Channel 4.'

CONTINUITY ANNOUNCER

'And now on BBC One, *Pointless*. Well, they said it.'

'There'll be more from *Embarrassing Bodies* next week. Now talking of unsightly twats, here's James Corden.'

'That programme was shown as a tribute to Vernon Kay who sadly is still not dead.'

'And now that thing with Nick Knowles in. God I hate him...'

'Just another three hours of pointless studio chat here on Sky before Grimsby–Sc*nthorpe finally kicks off.'

'It's Saturday evening on BBC One, so all you straight men can switch off.'

'If you've been affected by any of the issues raised in that programme – then please send for our factsheet "*Star Trek*'s Not Real".'

'Next on ITV, our new morning show *Daybreak*. This programme contains a puffy, grumpy Brummie face from the start.'

UNLIKELY PUZZLES

Spot the odd one out:

JANUARY	FEBRUARY	MARCH	TUESDAY	APRIL

Find a rhyme for this phrase: 'You are a sucking funt'.

Finish this million-piece jigsaw of a sand dune.

Take a look at this picture of five air stewards and out the odd one.

Before we ask you the puzzle question, we need to know your mother's maiden name and the first line of your address.

Using a pencil, draw a line from Arsène Wenger to where he is actually able to see an incident.

If it takes two men six weeks to devise cuts to tackle the country's deficit, how long will it take the Prime Minister to change them all when the public complain?

Rearrange the following in the same order:
GET A LIFE YOU LOSER

Look at these five pictures of holes and choose the one that will best accommodate the massive erect penis on the left.

Serial Killer Sudoku

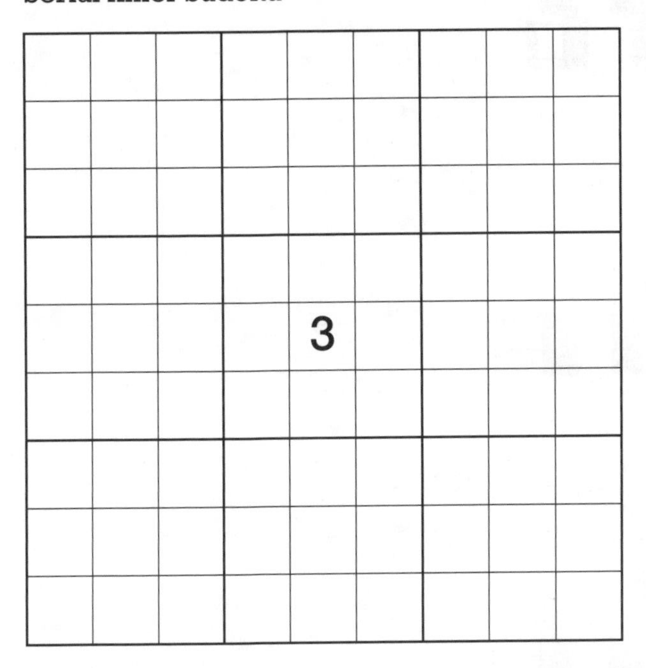

Beginner's Maze

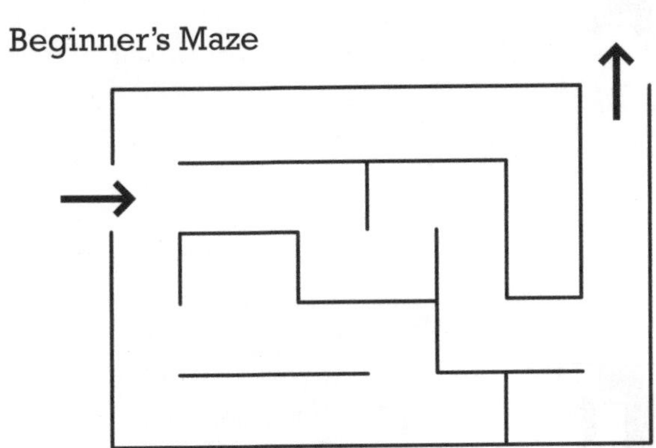

106 UNLIKELY COMPLAINTS TO T

Dear BBC, I had to watch last night's 'Dr Who' from behind the sofa, tugging myself off to his new assistant. Just thought you'd like to know.

Dear 'Points of View', just because my letter was sent from Essex doesn't mean you have to make me sound like a complete cock. Yours Amy Smith, aged eight.

My dad is a very bad actor. I can't believe you showed an episode of 'EastEnders' tonight which featured a lot of bad acting. How insensitive.

Why can't we have a documentary about the Second World War? This fascinating period in history is very unexplored.

Dear BBC, your religious coverage is not representative of all faiths. Why do we not see more naked Satanists sacrificing goats on BBC One primetime?

Dear sir – I wish to complain about the persistent dog fouling in my neighbourhood. I'm very short-sighted and may have got your address wrong.

Dear Channel XXX, the first ten minutes of this letter are free, if you want to read more than that, you'll have to pay.

Dear CBeebies, I strongly object to the latest edition of 'In the Night Garden' broadcast from Hampstead Heath.

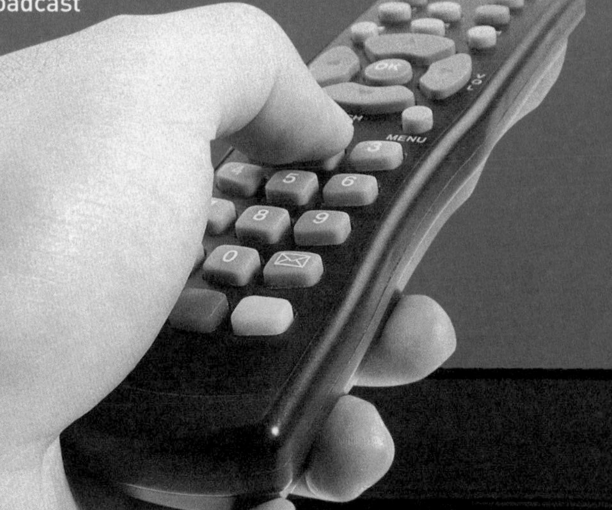

Dear Channel 4, last week I wrote asking if you could show more episodes of 'The Simpsons', I now understand that's literally not possible.

Dear Dave – has Mike been in? Brian.

Dear BBC, I'm fed up with the elitist intellectual ivory tower scheduling of BBC Three.

Dear MTV, I have been watching 'Teen Cribs'. I have come to the conclusion that all young people should be killed.

Dear sir, my children enjoyed 'Babe', and 'Babe 2: Pig in the City'. Imagine their disappointment when they tuned into your channel Babestation.

Dear Kerrang, I have turned the volume down to zero, and it's still too loud, please help.

Dear BBC, why oh why are we always looking for a new Dr Who when I understand the excellent Sylvester McCoy is currently available?

Dear Five + 1, why don't you call yourself Six?

'Springwatch' is just not the same without birdwatching Bill Oddie's amusing pun-based conversations about tits and shags.

Dear UK Gold + 1, I love your programmes, but they are on a little bit late for me. Could they be shown, say, an hour earlier?

Dear Babestation, I don't know what's going on, but last night, yet again, I couldn't hear a word the girls on the phones were saying.
Please sort it out.

Dear BBC Two, could you please arrange it so that when Nigella Lawson opens the fridge door for a midnight snack she's wearing something a lot more transparent than those frustrating pyjamas?

108 BAD THINGS TO SAY ON A FIRS

'Would you like to see a photograph of my children? Well, I say "my" children. I take pictures of them coming out of school.'

'I recently became a widower. Well, technically she's on life support, but it's the same thing really.'

'Don't be put off by the film crew – they're shooting a documentary called "When Psychopaths Date".'

'Yes, my Facebook photo was taken fifty years ago.'

'No, no, the meal's on me. Do you want a McFlurry for dessert?'

'Sorry, just got to send a quick tweet. How do you spell "minger"?'

'Yes, you're quite right – I was the cider-bottle player in The Wurzels.'

'You order the starters, I'll go to the toilet and get some condoms.'

'My last wife didn't understand me – she was Russian and I bought her off the Internet.'

'It all seems to be going very well. Do you want to come back to my caravan for coffee?'

'It's amazing you chose this restaurant, I had sex in this very car park last week.'

'I respect you and I'm not going to try anything on. And in any case I had a wank before I came out.'

'I'd buy you a drink, but then I thought sod it, she's got a job.'

'I'm not wearing underwear – I thought in this heat it would keep the flies off the food.'

'Have you got chlamydia? Only it would be miles easier if we both had it.'

'Goodness, I'm not a professional gynaecologist. More of an enthusiastic amateur.'

'I'm a big fan of Michael Jackson – I thought we should artificially inseminate for our children.'

'You're much taller than you look through that hole in your bathroom wall.'

'I'd like to see you again as often as possible – until the day you make me your passport-owning wife.'

'My parents live with me, well, I say "live".'

'I have to say you're looking absolutely gorgeous tonight, Mum – I mean Susan.'

'If you didn't want me looking down your top you shouldn't have worn one so low cut; anyway, I'd better get back to my date now.'

110 UNLIKELY VILLAGE NAMES

Wye-oh-Wye-oh-Wye
Lower Trousers
Steam-on-the-Piss
Wankersville
Clegg-under-Cameron
Property Hotspot
Cock-on-the-Curtain
Two Surnames
Lower Pissflaps
Heston Blumenthal
Frilly Under Wear
Little-Stains-on-the-Sheet
Greater Scape

TINCHY STRYDER 6

112 UNLIKELY GRAFFITI

I'm a talentless, angry twat

I, The Artist, declare that the above massive cock and balls are entirely my own work and were produced without the help of external parties

Vote Conservative

My Chalk Has Run Ou

Something Rude and Puerile

What You Staring At?

Jesus Saves!
He couldn't on my salary – or did you mean it in a religious sense?
Oh right, OK then I take it back

This wall is now available in paperback

Why is there never a piece of paper when you need one?

My mother made me a homosexual...
If I give her some wool, will she make me one?
... No, I mean her domineering attitude towards me meant she fucked up my sexuality and other areas of my psyche and I had to kill her in a horrible way...

No Graffiti By Order HM Govt.

Banksy is Shit

Photos of Me and You at the
Christmas Do, Posted On This Wall

The Juwes are not the men to be
blamed for nothing

Buy Ty Phoo Tea

If You Run Really Hard at
This Wall You Get to Hogwarts

Students Deesurve the
Best Educayshun

Immigrants Out! Unless They Possess an Exceptional Skill

CELTIC 3 RANGERS 0
St Mirren 0 Hibernian 1
Aberdeen 5 Kilmarnock 0
Hearts 2 Dundee United 1
Motherwell 1 Hamilton 0
Inverness Caledonian Thistle and St Johnstone is a late
kick- off

114 LINES THAT DIDN'T APPEAR I

'If you translate the Latin on that wall, then recite it backwards, it spells "You're All C*nts".'

Pausing for a moment, Professor Robert Langdon caught sight of his reflection in the mirror and pondered how much he looked like Forrest Gump.

'Oh my God! Look at this! Right under our feet! Bloody French poodles. It's gone all in the grooves of my trainers.'

'Sod the da Vinci Holy Grail conspiracy, professor – these guys are all kiddie fiddlers!'

'We'll solve this da Vinci code later,' said Langdon airily. 'First let's do this quick Sudoku.'

A thought suddenly struck Robert Langdon: 'Surely this is all bollocks?'

'I'll sort out the da Vinci code as soon as I've remembered the bloody password to my laptop.'

'I'll be late,' he said grimly. 'I'm watching Luton – Plymouth in the semi-final of the Sherpa Van Trophy.'

She explained it thus: 'In the year 1238, the Knights Templar killed all the Royal Family and dressed up straw men in their place.'
'Seems plausible,' he replied.

'Sorry, mate, Louvre's shut.'

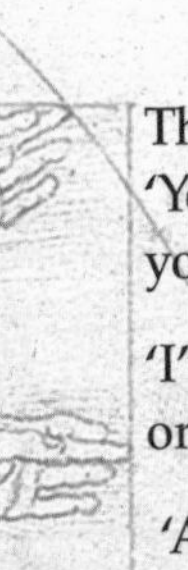

The priest's eyes bulged and his face reddened. 'You're supposed to wear the spiked garter on your leg,' said Langdon.

'I've read your work, Professor Langdon, and one word emerged in the text: "Shit".'

'Abracadabra!' said the professor. 'Door didn't open? Bollocks. That's that then.'

'I've uncovered an amazing secret about Jesus. His middle name began with an "H".'

'If you relax your eyes and look at "The Last Supper"...' the professor paused. 'Look, you can see two dolphins fighting!'

Hermione turned suddenly: 'Wow! I don't know what that last spell did, but I'm in a different book!'

'We can't do anything until the college opens in an hour,' he said.

'What do we do now? Wait?' Sophie asked.

'We could. Or...' As he spoke, the professor lazily parted his flies and flopped out his firm member. It pierced the air and Sophie seized it hungrily, urgently ... sorry, got carried away there.

'We need to get to a library quickly! These books are three weeks overdue.'

'How did you work that out, professor?' he asked.

'Easy, I just read the last page.'

In the dark forbidding silence of the cathedral, Robert Langdon farted.

116 UNLIKELY OBITUARIES

Peter Smith died peacefully in his sleep as he hurtled head-first through the windscreen of the car he was driving on the M6.

He had been one of the great guide dogs but was unfortunate to be given as his final posting an obscure and suicidal man who lived on the top floor of a tower block.

Serves him right for buying a hang-glider at Argos.

He may have been a regular member of the original *Star Trek* cast but sadly he neither lived particularly long, nor prospered.

Danny La Rue is survived by three children.

It is with some irony that a simple kung fu kick would have got David Carradine out of the wardrobe.

A memorial service is to be held tomorrow for Bert Scroggins, the inventor of weedkiller. No flowers, by request.

The tragic teenager was described by his headmaster as deeply unpopular, talentless and with no future whatsoever.

He never married, so in other words was an arse bandit.

He died of a mystery illness or 'Aids' as it's known to those outside his family that we don't want to offend.

Danny Dyer was an actor who I know I know just wishful

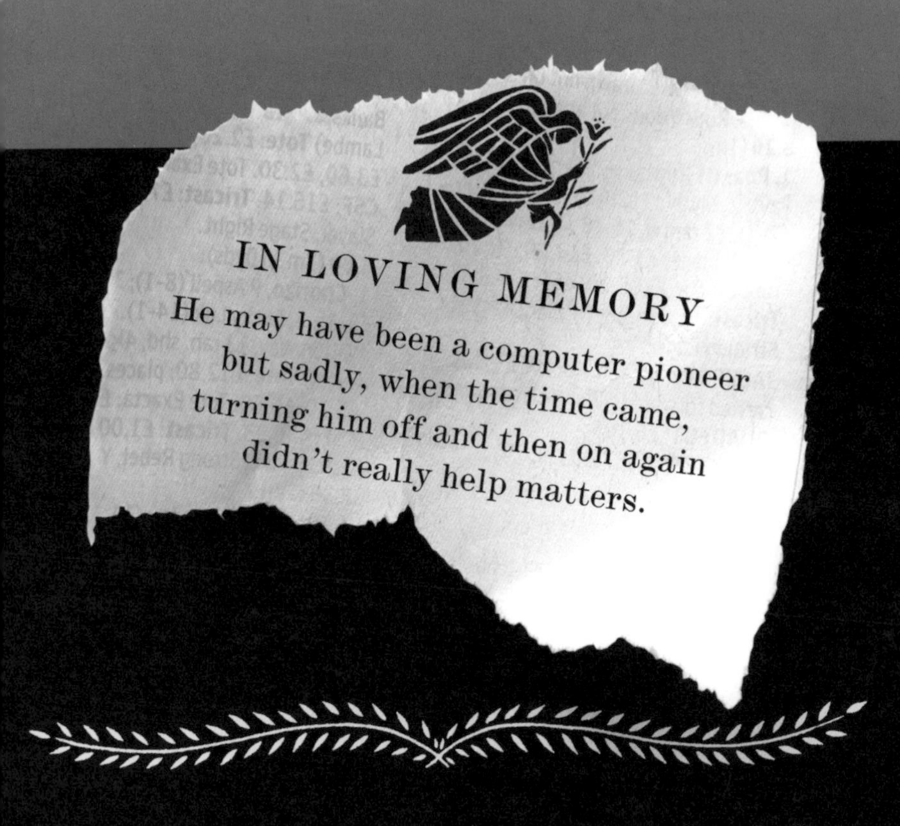

The death of TV advert star Barry Scott was sudden. In fact BANG! and the bloke was gone.

One of the world's wiliest footballers, it turned out the only thing he couldn't cheat was death.

Now then now then, howzabout that you see, God is a very busy man but he's finally come up trumps and fixed him for us.

He spent a great deal of time in London with his good friend Alexander Litvinenko.

Once again we will be running this Charlie Sheen obituary just to cover ourselves for tomorrow's early editions.

118 UNLIKELY THINGS TO HEAR O

'And as you can see, the ground is freezing ... just like the atmosphere in my bedroom.'

'You can tell these are French beans, they're arguing amongst themselves.'

'Well, there's a few bald patches on the grass at this time of year - so I'm going to grow it at the edges and then comb it over.'

'Then, holding the spade in both hands, slam it down on the mole's head...'

'My advice would be just to pour concrete over the whole thing and have done with it.'

'If you can't get hold of organic manure, I find a bowl of All-Bran and a good squat will do your roses a treat.'

'This peat is exceptionally moist - Peter, why are you so moist?'

'These ants can be difficult to get rid of - I find a flaming carpet of napalm works best.'

'With careful nurturing, and just the right amount of sun and water, a tomato plant should be bearing fruit within six months. That's why I can't be arsed and always buy mine from Tesco's.'

'We still have no idea who is sneaking into the allotment and adding topsoil. The plot thickens.'

'I've planted the seeds. I'm going to pop off to my shed now for a cup of tea and a look through my collection of eye-watering porn.'

'Please help - I'm growing genetically modified geraniums and - No! They ... the door ... aaaargh!'

GARDENING PROGRAMME

'It was in a patch of nasturtiums, just like these beautiful blooms here, that I first got my end away as a teenager.'

'Over there are a spade and a dirty hoe ... are we still on air?'

'At the start of this series, I promised that I would live only on natural fruits and vegetables that I grew myself. And that's why I've lost five stone, all my teeth, and my wife.'

'I've eaten as many strawberries as I can. So now it's time to take the box to the counter and pay for the rest of them.'

'Welcome to *Gardening for Beginners*. This week, we're looking at potato trees.'

'Three weeks in and I'm still living off stuff from the allotment. Tonight - dead fox.'

'Now this is one of my favourite Roses - a chocolate toffee.'

'The best way to get rid of those irritating garden pests is to give them their own chat show.'

'And Charlie's going to really get down and bed these bulbs in while I look down her top and Tommy tries to get a gander at her arse crack.'

'Oh, and some nightshade there - completely harmless and tastes absolutely ... Oh my God, call an ambulance, call an ambulance for Christ's sake!'

120 UNLIKELY VEGAS HOTELS

THE BUBONIC
THE CROYDON
TRAFFIC ISLAND
MINGERS'
THE BELLENDIO
THE TERRORIST TARGET
BATES MOTEL
9/11
THE HARD COCK ON THE STRIP
THE LOADED DICE
THE MASSIVE SLOT
THE BANKRUPTIO
THE DFS GRAND
THE INDELIBLE STAIN
THE RITZ CRACKER
SHAGGERS ON THE BEACH
THE STAIN ON THE CARPET
SHITTERS

UNLIKELY CONDOM BRANDS

STRAWBERRY SPLIT
HOGWARTS
WIDDECOMBE'S ORIGINAL
CHEESE AND PICKLE
FLOPPY
POROUS
ARMED RUBBER
THE JIZZ CATCHER 3000
THE THISTLE
THE BORIS
DEREK
SPERMINATOR
PUSSY POUNDER
FUN SIZE MICRO MAN SHEATH
REVERSIBLE RUBBER
THE SUSAN BOYLE FEMIDOM RANGE
THE QWIKIE FIT ON AND IN
THE LANE CHANGER XTRA STRONG

122 THINGS YOU WON'T HEAR WHEN FLICKI

'To get to the end of your wank, switch over to Red Hot 2 now. Here on Red Hot 1, the news and weather.'

'And now a documentary about something other than sharks, Nazis or Ancient Egypt.'

'Welcome to Channel X. You're watching ... your mum.'

'Let's go over and see what pathetic excuse John Terry will be cobbling together for this week's fuck up.'

'Next on the Biography Channel, the Don Estelle story.'

'Welcome to ITV 7 ... no, we didn't know it went up that high either.'

'Coming up next, James Alexander Gordon reads today's Premier League football scores whilst a topless housewife fellates a black dildo.'

'Coming up next on E4: *Friends – The One Where You Realize That It's Not as Funny as It Used to Be*.'

'You're watching Challenge TV, where the challenge is to try and get your fat arse off the sofa.'

'Now on More 4, our new sister channel: What The Fuck 4.'

'After watching *Jonathan Creek* on BBC3, why not watch it again on BBC3+1 and impress your friends by guessing who did it?'

'No, don't keep flicking, wait ... I used to be on Channel 4 ... stop, come back!'

'Welcome to Facebook TV. Yep, it's come to that.'

ROUGH SATELLITE TV

'And allow me to introduce pundit Phil Thompson, and pause whilst everyone at home says "Look at the size of that conk!"'

'Welcome to Sky One, where you'll find the biggest names in comedy and the smallest audiences in television.'

'Welcome to *Where are they Now? Dad's Army Special*. Well, they're pretty much all dead actually.'

'Welcome to another edition of *After They Were Famous* or, as you call it, ITV 2.'

'Hope you've got your penis and tissue paper handy. Here is the Ten Minute Freeview.'

124 UNLIKELY THINGS TO READ O

I said 'Open other *end', for fuck's sake! – now get a dustpan and brush.*

Chocolate animals – do not eat if seal is broken.

If you've enjoyed this Innocent Smoothie, why not write to us, here at Fruit Towers, or email us at irritating,whimsicaltwats.com.

May contain human urine – well, wouldn't you if you worked in a factory all day?

Contains tender chunks of lamb in a delicious sauce, or cat food depending on which day it is.

Organic lettuce – or so we claim.

Please drink this half-price, six-pack of strong lager responsibly.

Serves four, you fat bastard – put the rest back.

Assembly requires two people, and a working knowledge of Swedish.

Scottish broth – warning, contains vegetables.

Spam fritters – best before D-Day.

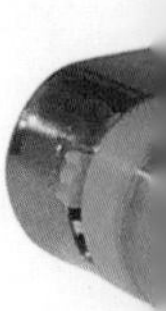

Diplomat
Smoking may cause cancer, but it'll take ages and until then you'll look cool.

126 UNLIKELY THINGS TO HEAR O

'The victim is Eamonn Holmes – I think we may need some more chalk.'

'We've gone over the corpse with a fine toothcomb and she looks lovely now with that centre parting.'

'The murdered man was a bit of a twat, so let's just give up and go home.'

'Sssh, everyone, Miss Marple is about to tell us who the murderer is ... Miss Marple, that's you ... no, we've had tea ...'

'I see you've traded in your Jaguar, Morse, for a Nissan Micra.'

'Forty-eight hours? Nonsense! You take as long as you like. I mean, it's not as if I've got the DA's office on my back, or anything.'

'Introducing Detective Inspector Brian Sod in *Sod's Law*.'

'The skin seems flushed around the face and there would appear to be traces of semen on the breasts – for which, darling, I can only apologize.'

'Frost, you ruined the stakeout. When you were meant to arrest the criminal you fell through the hatch in the bar.'

'Rosemary, it's an emergency, someone wants to buy a plant at our garden centre.'

'Well, that's it, there's nobody left alive in Midsomer.'

'Well, our hour's nearly up, we're going to have to file this under "Unsolved".'

'When I said "Can you identify the body?" I didn't mean you to say "He's the dead bloke over there."'

DETECTIVE SHOW

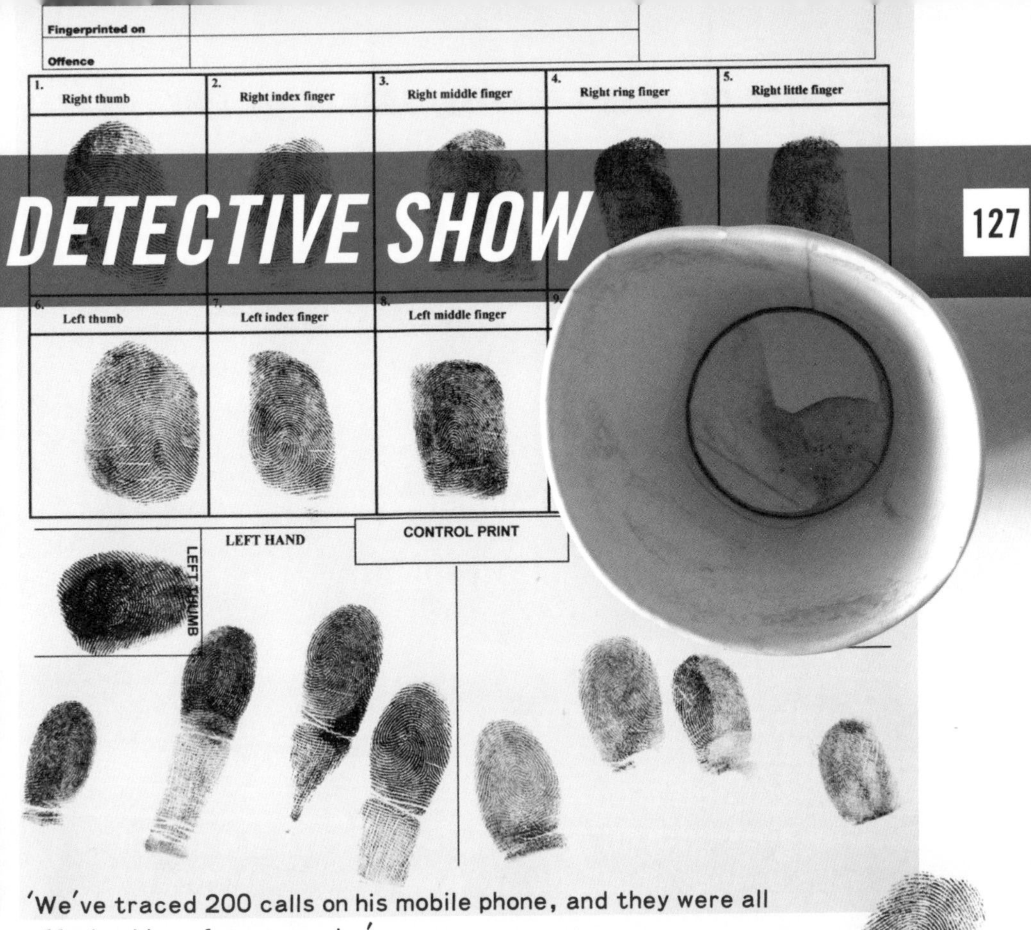

'We've traced 200 calls on his mobile phone, and they were all offering him a free upgrade.'

'We've analysed the laptop and it's full of pornography ... hang on, that's my laptop.'

'Oh you said "WAKING the dead". Sorry, what must you think of me?'

'In the criminal justice system, the people are represented by two separate yet equally important groups: the police who investigate crime and the quiz-show hosts like Bradley Walsh. These are their stories. Come on down, it's *Law & Order: UK*.'

'You can't just pin it on the black guy, Barnaby, remember? This is Midsomer, they aren't allowed here.'

'It seems to be some sort of code. Morse.'

'Is this show called *Waking the Dead* because all Trevor Eve does is bellow through every episode?'

UNLIKELY THINGS TO READ O

Tired? Just close your eyes for five minutes and relax

Warning! Middlesbrough ahead

Workmen in road ahead. Just drive over the c*nts

Welcome to Hell

Terrible modernist architecture ahead. Don't Look

Beware children playing in road. It's a council estate, they've all got knives

No camera section – we'll just trust you

Accident on other carriageway. Please slow down and gawp

George Michael asleep on hard shoulder

Smile, you're on *Police, Camera, Action!*

GM strawberries ahead – they'll pick themselves!

Italy welcomes careless drivers

MOTORWAY SIGN

UNLIKELY THINGS TO HEAR A

'I've done the turkey Nigella style, by which I mean while I cooked it your dad had a wank.'

'Either we've been burgled, or all Dad's got us is a big turd on the carpet.'

'OK, so we're here for the footie match, but where are the Hun?'

'Sorry there's no crown in your cracker, Charles.'

'We'll make "Debbie Does Dallas" the last charade, Granny.'

'On this seasonal special of *Countryfile* we take a heart-warming look at the journey of a turkey, from battery farm to slaughterhouse.'

'Here you go, son, I got you some porn so you'll stop looking at your sister in the shower.'

'I wish Grandad was with us this year. But he's run off with the woman down the road.'

'Look, Santa's come - and he's wiped his cock on my stocking.'

'I know you want to get your secretary a present, but wrapping a ribbon round your penis and lying under the tree isn't really in the Christmas spirit.'

'Next on BBC Two, *How to Cook Turkey Giblets* ... oh, sorry, it's *Madonna Live in Concert*.'

'Philip and I have had an eventful 2007, I got an intimate piercing and he is loving his Nintendo Wii shoot-'em-up game.'

'Now, live from St Dunstan's in Suffolk - hoodies nicking lead off the roof.'

'You remember I told you Dad died in his canoe...?'

'And now a seasonal message from Richard Dawkins.'

'The following programme contains nudity. I'd set the video for forty-seven minutes in.'

'I couldn't get Lego Star Wars, so I got Death Rampage 3.'

'Time for charades. Me and your mum are going to pretend we're still happily married while the neighbours come round for a drink.'

'Now, with a special seasonal edition, *CSI Lapland*.'

'This year we're having an alternative to turkey, who wants a paw?'

'Here's the bike you wanted, son. It has to be back in its docking port by six.'

'Don't forget, kids, to write your special letter to the man who makes all our presents come - the President of China.'

'Now in *EastEnders*, someone gets pregnant, the pub burns down, blah blah blah, you've seen it all before.'

132 THINGS YOU WON'T HEAR O

'You can tell which are the counterfeit notes, because the Queen has her cock out.'

'We've had five calls so far: one from a double-glazing firm, two from a kitchen company, one from the wife about dinner and a wrong number.'

'And now CCTV. Here are the top ten off-licence robberies this month. Choose which one you think is the best and if our panel agree you can win a month's supply of WKD.'

'The suspect was caught on CCTV cameras – unfortunately, he's a CCTV camera thief.'

'Oi! – someone's nicked my sandwich!'

'Now here's Rav with the CCTV footage, as we gradually give him less and less to do each week, because though he looks nice, he couldn't present his way out of a paper bag.'

'Have nightmares.'

'In the early hours of this morning, a forty-nine-year-old man broke into number 7, The Lanes, Swindon, and tried to gain entry to the master bedroom. He was attacked and repeatedly beaten by the owner and forced to sleep in the spare room again. Do you think there is anything wrong with a man going out for a few beers with his mates to watch the footy? If not, email my wife at this address.'

'For years Nick Ross was comfortable in this job – then I nicked it off him.'

'Hey, you remember those people we told you about last week? We caught them.'

'Due to budget cuts, this week's reconstruction uses conkers with felt-tip faces drawn on.'

'We've had four calls so far and they've all been to say my flies were undone during that chat with Kirsty. Sorry about that.'

134 UNLIKELY TITLES FOR MEMOIRS

KINNOCK KINNOCK, WHO'S THERE?: Glenys Kinnock

WHY WON'T SHE JUST FUCKING DIE CHARLES: MY STORY

IT'S FINE AND I DIDN'T WANT THE STUPID JOB ANYWAY: David Miliband

THE BLAIR NECESSITIES, POPPING THE CHERIE AND CHERIE ON TOP: THE TONY BLAIR OMNIBUS COLLECTION

LOOK BACH IN ANGER: COLLECTED LETTERS VOLUME 2: J. S. Bach

JACKING OFF: Jacqui Smith
The sensational sequel to *PORN FREE*

CHICO - THE WONDER YEARS

CLUTCHING AT STRAWS: Jack Straw

FUCK OFF THE LOT OF YOU: Wayne Rooney

HOW AM I FAMOUS AGAIN?: Kim Kardashian

BIRDS, BOOZE AND MAN STUFF: William Hague

A COLONEL OF TRUTH: Muammar Gaddafi

THATCHER
IN THE
RYE

MARGARET
THATCHER

THE EARLY YEARS

UNLIKELY LINES FROM A JAMES BOND BOOK

Chapter 12

'I'm going to have to deal with the bomb manually,' said Bond. 'Now when I hit it with the hammer, run like fuck.'

'You might find, Bond, at the lowest point in the mission, you'll have to press this button – it's the fast-forward.'

'Here's your new jetbike, Bond. When you've finished with it, just put it in any of Boris's docking stations.'

The telephone continued to ring, taunting Bond. He knew he had only a matter of seconds to answer it, but with his ankles bound together it took an age to shuffle through to the other room. With a final, desperate lunge, he knocked the handset from its cradle and slid his face to it. 'Can I call you back, M?' he gasped. 'I'm on the crapper.'

The young James Bond took out his ordinary looking fountain pen, which turned into a sippy-cup…

'Right, I'll try the blue wire first … and if the fairy lights still don't come on we'll get some new bulbs.'

Bond looked out of the window as he crossed the Thames. The morning sun dappled the river like an Impressionist painting, an empty tourist boat meandered towards a sparsely populated jetty ahead of its first run of the day and the sounds of lapping water and distant motors transported him first to Cuba, then China, finally outer space. His sharp mind temporarily formed a picture book of memories his work had bought him: glamour, brutality, wonder … Bond had seen it all, but now it was time to don his false beard and hat and spend a 300th consecutive day hiding in a cupboard in Finsbury Park Mosque with a fucking tape recorder.

Slowly, deliberately, with practised care, Bond wiped away a bead of sweat and opened the box. 'Oh for fuck's sake, I ordered anchovies,' he said.

138 UNLIKELY SUPERHEROES

PROFESSOR PISSPANTS
CAPTAIN BALLET
TOLLUND MAN
WONDERBRA WOMAN
THE BRIAN KID
DR DRIZZLE
MILK MAN
FLASHER
SUPER KEVIN PHILLIPS
FUCKWIT
X-WIFE
FATHERS FOR JUSTICE
IRONING MAN
LADY GARDEN
CAPTAIN GROPE
BADLY MARKETED MAN
PAUL
THE PROSTATE KID

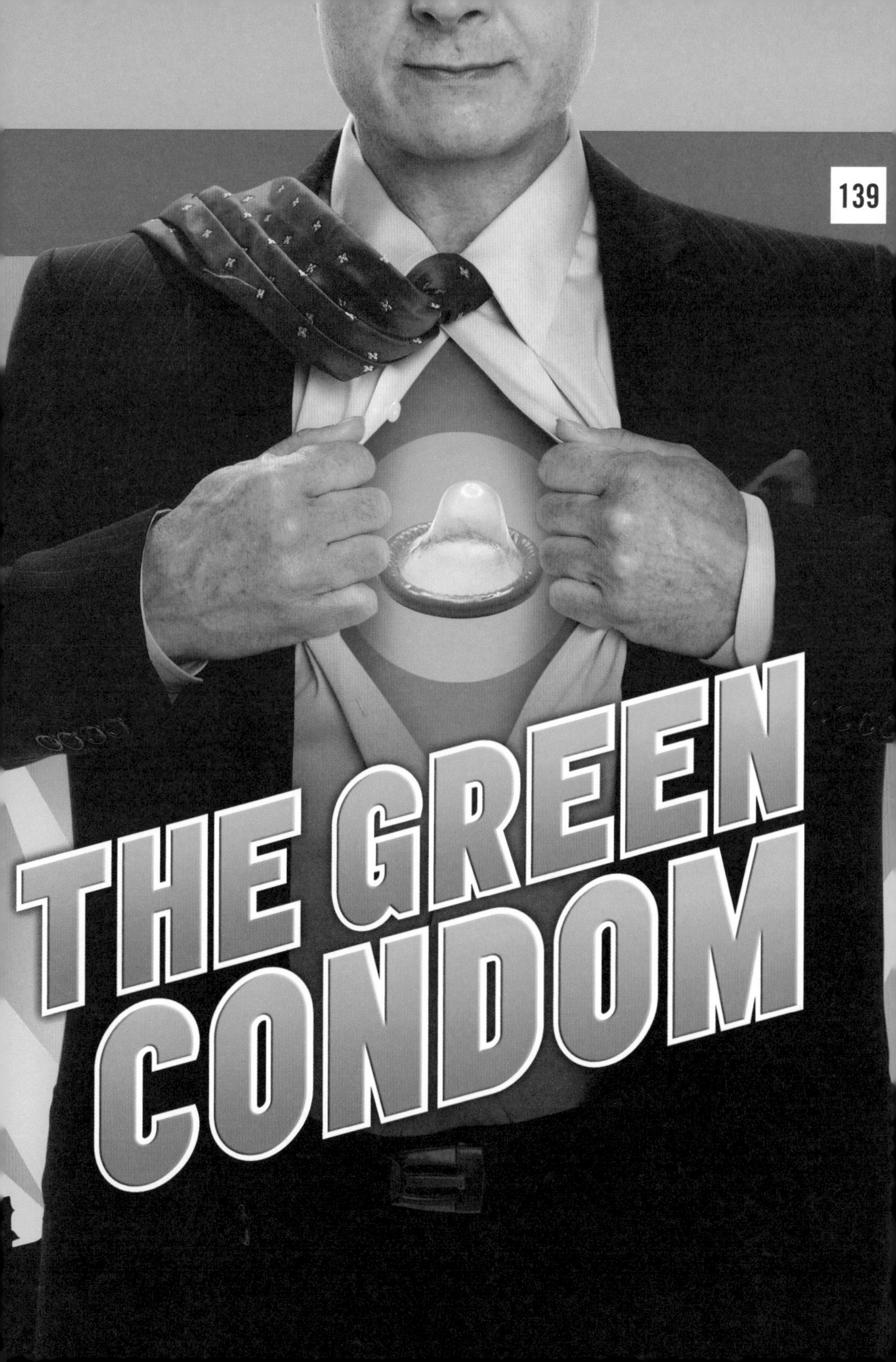

THE GREEN CONDOM

UNLIKELY INSTRUCTIONS FO

The game is considered finished when Daddy has a tantrum and kicks the board across the room.

Included inside are all but one of the cards you need to play this game.

How to play Chinese Checkers – put more and more pieces on the board until you've taken over the world.

Pass Go and do not collect £200 as the government have axed the 'passing go and collecting £200' benefit.

Professor Plum, up the bum with some lead piping in the library. Yes, it's Rude-o.

Kerplunk! I hate it when the ceiling collapses during a game of Scrabble.

OK, your first question in Trivial Pursuit – you're playing for: a) a piece of cake; b) a wedge of cheese; c) a piece of pie; or d) just a shit plastic triangle?

Welcome to Republican Chess. No king or queen and the castle has been turned into a workers' cafeteria.

To escape from jail roll two sixes or wait for the government to announce an amnesty.

Please note that the piece illustrated here is known as a knight, and not 'a horsey'.

You've bought Ludo. Maybe one day your parents will get a television, but in the meantime here are the rules.

BOARD GAME

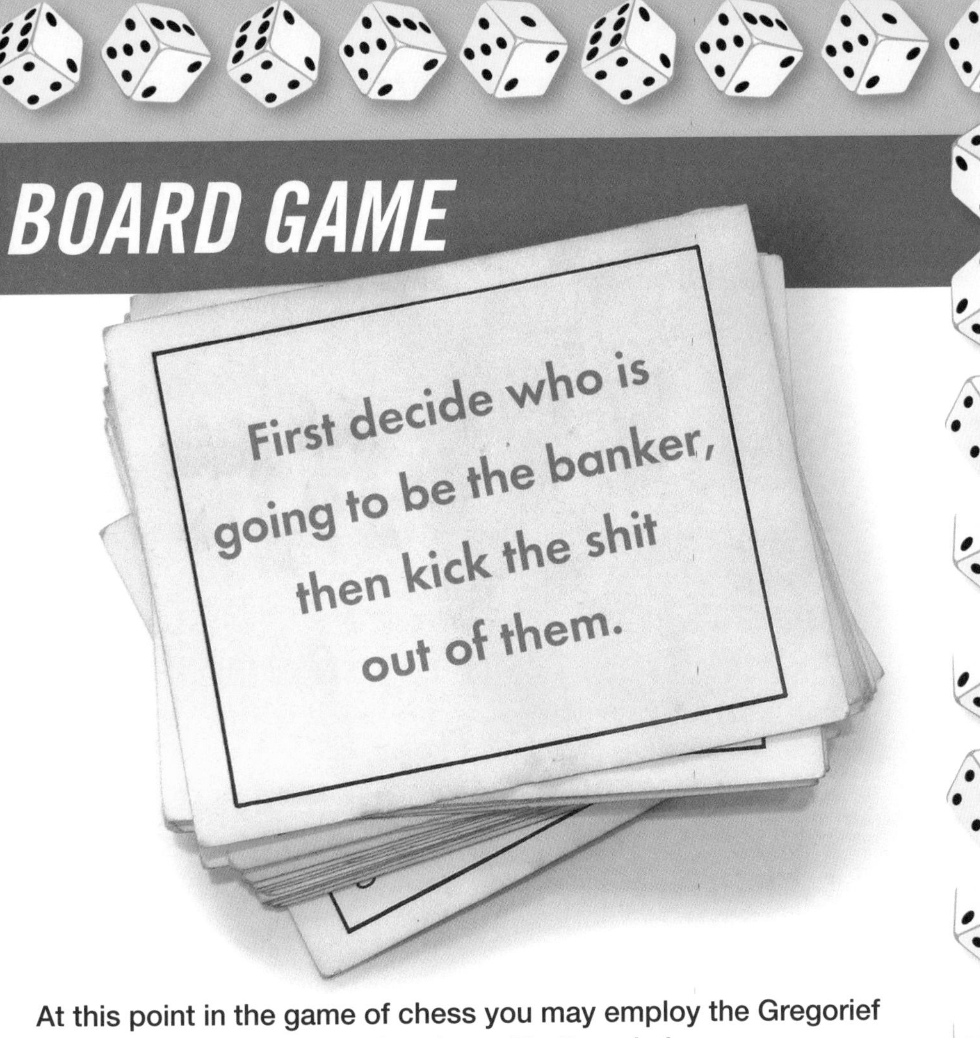

At this point in the game of chess you may employ the Gregorief defence – knock the board and say 'Earthquake'.

Oh no, I've landed on a snake … I hate having to play chess in the jungle.

The players must take it in turns to steal money from the banker when he goes to the toilet.

At this point Uncle Frank will make the comment: 'If only property in Mayfair was £400.' Players should then laugh politely.

Operation – oh no, the patient's died of MRSA.

Chapter 12 • *Miscellaneous*

• If you jump from a building over 600 feet tall and wear a large flapping coat, you will almost certainly live.

• Bobby Charlton was actually bald and his 'hair' was, in reality, a long side bit he combed over to cover up his head

• In many Asian countries, *Top Gear* is called 'Manna Wan Choowa' which translates as 'Those Three C*nts and Some Cars'.

• Heather Mills has over one hundred single left shoes.

• The sun is 9 inches across.

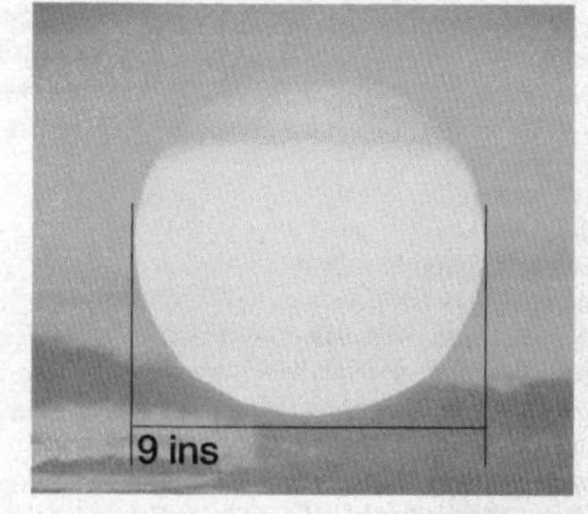

• The Apollo moon landings were faked. The scenes were actually filmed on Mars.

• The Queen and Prince Charles are actually the same person, which is why they never fly together.

• One tomato a day guarantees immortality.

• England didn't actually win the World Cup in 1966, the whole thing was an elaborate practical joke for a German 'hidden camera' TV show.

• Your head is stronger than an iron bar. (Go on. Do it.)

• There are no bicycles in Beijing.

• Cheese is fish.

• Richard the Lionheart did survive for several months with the transplanted heart of an African lion.

• Contrary to popular myth, Marianne Faithfull was not using a Mars Bar in a sex game when Keith Richards's house was raided by police. It was actually a Snickers (or Marathon as it was then called).

• There is no substance known to humanity that actor Charlie Sheen has not ingested on a night out.

• The rules of the Eton Wall Game can only be understood by homosexuals.

• Leigh Delamere invented the motorway service station.

• The word paedophile comes from the Greek work 'paedo' meaning 'Gary' and the Latin word 'phile' meaning 'Glitter'.

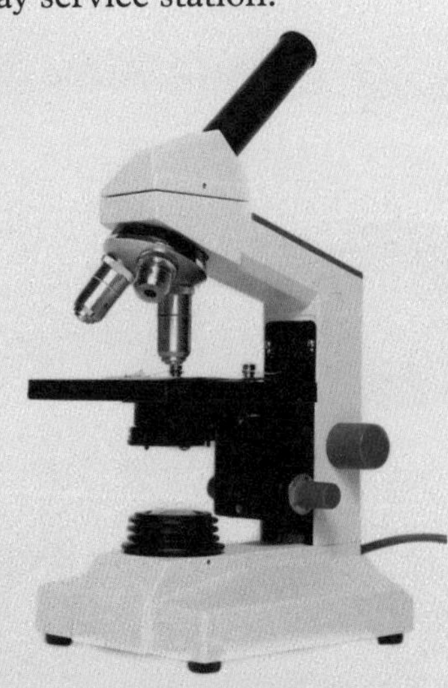

• Peter Kay is not Vernon Kay's brother. They actually used to be married.

• Dermot O'Leary is so small he is only visible to the naked eye by using a series of powerful microscopes and lasers.

144 BAD TITLES FOR LOVE SONGS

'My Dog's Got Worms'

'You've Got the Smallest Human Cock I've Ever Seen'

'Have You Finished?'

'Undo These Cuffs'

'I'm Just a Sweet Chiropodist from Luton'

'I Can't Help Pulling You Off'

'Go On Then, You'll Do'

'The First Time Ever I Saw Your Tits'

'Don't Make Me Come Over There'

'I Just Came In Your Arms Tonight'

'I'm All Out of Spunk'

'When a Man Loves a Wombat'

'You Put Your Finger Up My Arse'

'My Penis Is Weeping'

TOTAL ECLIPSE
SIDE A
45 RPM CRACK69
MADE IN ENGLAND
OF YOUR ARSE

UNLIKELY INDEX

Index

148 UNLIKELY NAMES FOR BREAKFAS

Hitler's Honey and Nut Flakes

Corn Scratchings

Fruit and Nut Coalition

Raisins, Hazelnuts, Sultanas, Shit

Screaming Puffs

Kellogg's Doner Kebab

Crunchy Foot Corn Flakes

Just Fucking Sugar

Poo Pops

New Wholegrain...
LAMB POPS
They're Baa-rilliant!
8 Essential Vitamins

150 UNLIKELY CENSUS QUESTION

1. Where do you live? What's it like? Is it nice?
2. What's a nice girl like you doing answering a census like this?
3. You speakee, speakee English, no?
4. How long's yer knob then?
5. To answer the next question, please get on board a donkey and take your family to a stable in Bethlehem.
6. How's the family? Is your Janet still in the same place?
7. Would you mind just popping your things off for me?
8. Have you ever or are you now harbouring a Nazi war criminal?
9. What are you fucking looking at?
10. What football team do you support? If you could buy one player from another team who would it be?

11 What is your job? Do you do it outdoors? Could I do it?

12 Me and my husband feel the spark has gone out of our marriage. Have you any tips for spicing things up in the bedroom?

13 How many children have you got? How many? *What*? Have you not heard of johnnies?

14 What colour was your most recent stool?

15 Put The Saturdays in the order you would shag them.

16 Think of a number. Double it. OK. Fuck off that many times.

17 Who are you pretending to be today?

18 How many pints can you drink? Oh yeah? Come on, then, let's see it.

19 How many sexual partners have you had? Attach photos if pos.

20 Lembit Öpik – discuss.

21 How many people are there in your house, right now? No, you haven't looked in the attic.

22 Ethnicity. Are you dusky?

LINES YOU WON'T HEAR I

'Are all Vulcans circumcised?'

'It's Michael Jackson - he's dead, Jim.'

'Hello, Darth, what brings you here?'

'Which idiot put a red ***Star Trek*** top in the wash with all the yellow ones?'

'To be honest, you were better in ***Spaced*** and ***Shaun of the Dead***.'

Captain's blog. OMG - Just seen the aliens - LOL

'It's a fan club convention, Mr Spock. Take evasive action immediately.'

'We are approaching a barren featureless wasteland with no signs of intelligent life - Basingstoke.'

'OK new regulations - before I beam you down you have to hand over any liquids over 100 ml.'

'Who's set my phasar to vibrate again? Was it you, Uhura?'

'OK so you win again at 3D chess, Spock, but let's see how you do on ***Grand Theft Auto***.'

'We find ourselves on the mysterious planet Polystyrenia.'

'Beam me up, Scotty. Oh shit, I haven't paid my bill and I've been disconnected.'

'Get a mechanic to the bridge, our slidey doors have stopped making the WHOOSH WHOOSH noise.'

'I'm not an Orthodox Vulcan.'

'I'm afraid we have a waiting list for the sickbay – it's seven light years.'

'Don't shoot. It's the pizza delivery boy.'

'Have you ever noticed that 95 per cent of all alien life in this universe is composed of humans in rubber costumes?'

154 UNLIKELY COSMETICS COMMERCIA

Dove Cosmetics – for fat biffers like these

A cream that fights wrinkles day and night … to absolutely no effect

The secret to my younger-looking skin? – spunk!

Maybe she's born with it, maybe it's Maybelline, either way she probably needs to get it looked at, it's not right, is it?

As used by Mother Teresa

Gillette – the best a man can get and the first thing a woman borrows to do her legs

It drives men wild, which isn't a massive-selling point for an aftershave

If a man you've never met before suddenly gives you flowers, he's probably a sex attacker

Because underneath all this I'm an absolute minger

Comes with free trowel and sander

For Her. (But she won't know if you have a dabble when she's out – you know you want to)

See where it takes you … probably the Burns Unit

Hi, I'm Lady Gaga and I'm here to talk to you about the Remington Ear and Nose Hair Trimmer

Maybe she's born with it, maybe she's plastered her face in a two-inch-thick layer of slap

Nivea – for when you're more than just pig ugly

Right Guard – for 24-hour protection, or you could just wash a bit more

'I, Dr John Watson, beg leave to speak to you here of "The Reigate Puzzle". Namely: Why the fuck would anyone want to live there?'

'Watson, you know my success is based on the observation of trifles and I can safely state that you've put far too much fucking sherry in this one.'

Later, at dinner, we talked over our host's incredible success in 'The Case of the Guildford Four'. 'Inspector...' said Holmes with a wry grin, 'nothing clears up a case so much as fabricating evidence and forging a confession.'

'I perceive that you had marmalade for breakfast this morning, Watson,' Holmes said as I walked into his rooms that sunny June morning.

'As ever, Holmes, your powers of deduction are quite remarkable,' I stammered.

'You've got it all over your trousers, you fuckwit,' he said, resuming his perusal of the paper.

Holmes heard mention of the name 'Irene Adler' and he paused, as I knew he would, lost in contemplation as he looked out of the room's smallest window, just to his left. To Holmes, she was always the woman. It was not that he felt any emotion akin to love for her; just that she had once tugged him off in the back of a hansom cab and was what he called 'The Cleopatra of tits'.

158 BAD THINGS TO HEAR IN HOSPITA

I've had a good look at your breasts, Mrs Smith – so now I can get on with painting the ward.'

'I think I can do this rectal exam quickly, if I just pull my finger out.'

'I'd like you to count slowly backwards from 300. The timer on the microwave's broken.'

'OK, pay attention, students, this next lesson is very important. Milk, milk, lemonade, round the corner chocolate's made.'

'Nurse – the curtains! She's coming round and I've got nowhere to wipe my cock.'

'I'm normally the porter for the mortuary ... anyway, maybe see you again soon!'

'Of course the NHS isn't short of drugs. If you'd just like to chew on this piece of parsley while I grind up the tree-bark.'

'You don't mind if our work experience kids have a bash at your appendectomy?'

'You haven't eaten your dinner. This organization does not tolerate failure...'

'Oh come on, I see men's willies every day, Mr Johns, although admittedly not as small as yours.'

'Now here's a funny thing about Dr Jenkins. In his handwriting the words "tonsils" and "genitals" look almost identical.'

'While you're asleep, Dr Jones will be removing your organ from your body ... and I will be putting mine in.'

'Just sign these forms absolving me from any liability in the event of this operation going hideously wrong ... again.'

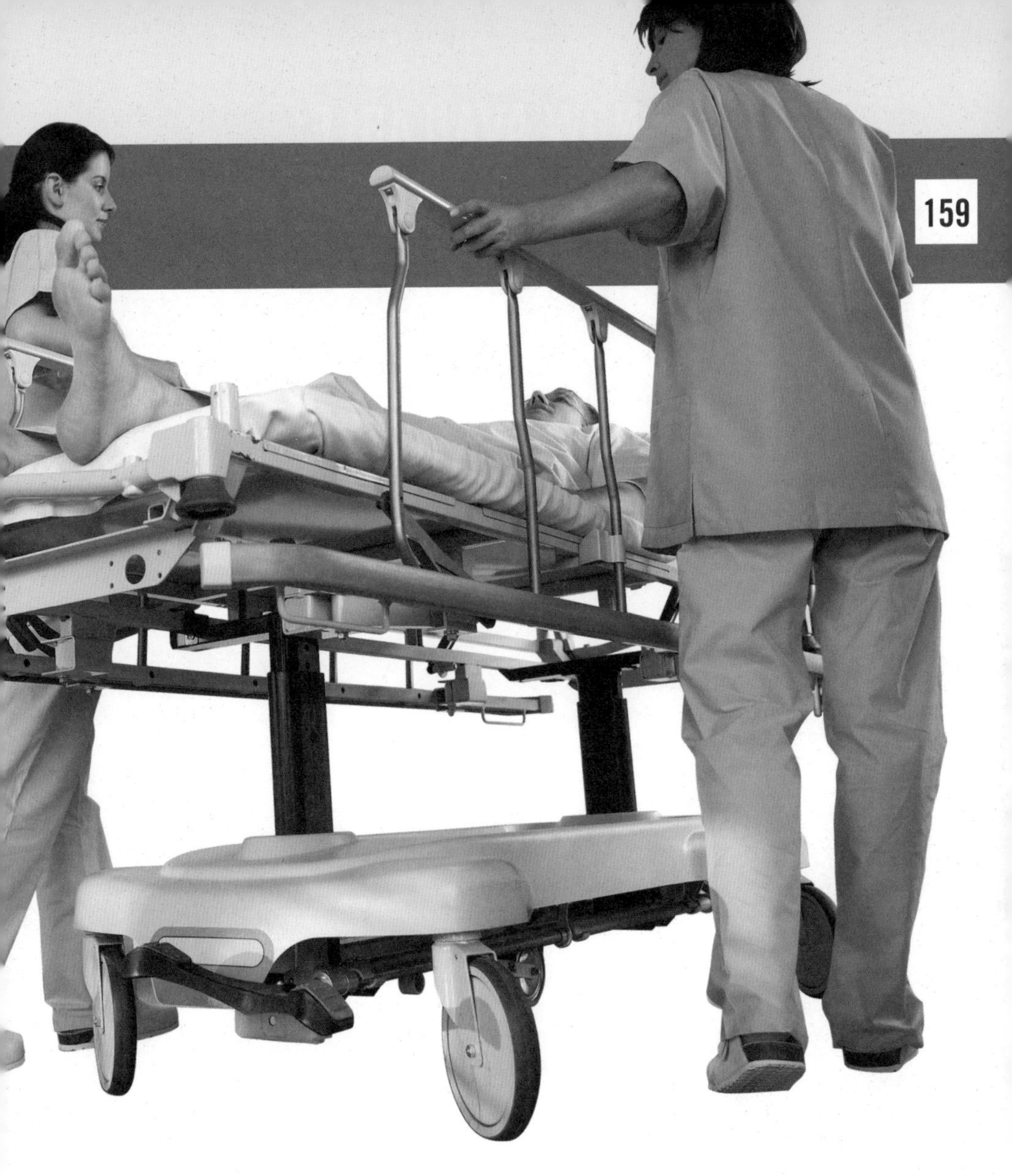

'Hello Sir Alex. Just before we do your colonoscopy allow me to introduce the operating team. Coincidentally we're all either Liverpool or Man City fans.'

'It's a very quick operation these days, now put your hands in these manacles and bite down on the piece of wood whilst I line up the hacksaw. Nurse! The rum!'

MOCK
THE
WEEK